AF477243

Learn R. By coding.

Copyright

Title book: Learning R. By coding.
Author book: Thomas Kurnicki

© 2019, Thomas Kurnicki
Self publishing
ISBN 978-83-952046-1-6

Dedicated to ...

Students...
And anyone else who understands the importance of data.

Table of Contents

Preface

First of all, I have to thank my wife for showing me a lot of support in writing this book. She always made references to the fact that learning a new coding language is just as hard as learning polish for a foreigner. This inspired me to help students practice R and create a repository of examples and exercises that boost the learning curve.

I'd also like to thank CC and XX. Both of them motivated me to study mathematics and enhance my coding skills. They've contributed many countless hours to my development.

This book is created for students and working professionals that are at the beginning of their journey with R. Prior experience or education in statistics or skills in another programming language is a "good-to-have" as this book will explain basic data manipulation, modeling, and programming frameworks. However, this book takes the reader from step one so that anyone, even without prior experience, can understand the content.

Each chapter will outline basic concepts and challenges and provide countless examples and exercises for each topic. It is highly recommended to follow the order of chapters as further chapters require understanding of the previous content. At the end of this book, the user should be able to create web applications and dashboards in Shiny.

Some readers might be disappointed due to the limited usage of buzz-words. "Machine learning, deep learning, and artificial intelligence" are avoided at all cost. Instead, the reader will receive a better understanding of basic programming concepts and will be exposed to more exercises and hands-on examples.

1. R intro: the environment

1.1 Short passage about R

From the R project website (source: https://www.r-project.org/about.html):

> *R provides a wide variety of statistical (linear and nonlinear modelling, classical statistical tests, time-series analysis, classification, clustering, …) and graphical techniques, and is highly extensible. The S language is often the vehicle of choice for research in statistical methodology, and R provides an Open Source route to participation in that activity.*
>
> *One of R's strengths is the ease with which well-designed publication-quality plots can be produced, including mathematical symbols and formulae where needed. Great care has been taken over the defaults for the minor design choices in graphics, but the user retains full control.*
>
> *R is available as Free Software under the terms of the Free Software Foundation's GNU General Public License in source code form. It compiles and runs on a wide variety of UNIX platforms and similar systems (including FreeBSD and Linux), Windows and MacOS.*

As noted on the R-project website, R is the ultimate language for data scientists, statisticians, physicists, and many other professionals that need to work with data and want to make their lives easier.

1.2 Installation

In order to run R programs, you need to install the R compiler from the R-project website. The following URL works as of July 2018: https://cran.r-project.org/mirrors.html

This link has a list of all R mirrors. Find the location that is closest to your location and click on the URL. This will take you to the nearest CRAN (Comprehensive R Archive Network) and will list all available operating systems for which R is available. Download the one that will work with your operating system. After the download is complete, follow the prompts

If the link listed above doesn't work, use one of the popular search engines like www.google.com and search for R CRAN. The results should give you the most current URL under which the R CRAN is hosted.

1.2.1 R Studio installation

Even though having R from the CRAN is sufficient to run R programs on your local computer, you might want to consider using an IDE (Integrated Development Environment) to develop your code.

R Studio is so far, the best (according to the author) free IDE available today. It has many useful features such as:

- Matching special characters in your code, closing functions,
- Accessing all objects in the global and local environments,
- Browsing all plots created in the current R session.

R Studio is available from the following website: https://www.rstudio.com

There are a few versions of R Studio, including a commercial version for which the user has to pay. However, there is an open source version that is free and easy to download. All of the versions are available in the product section on the website.

1.2.2 Installation verification

For the first time you open R Studio, it will show 3 windows. We will explain the functionalities of all the windows in the next chapter.

In the big window on the left-hand side, called the 'console', type "Hello World" (you will notice that when opening the quotations, R Studio will automatically close them for you) and click enter. This will submit the "Hello World" statement.

This submission should result in the following response (printed in the next line):

[1] "Hello World"

If you see the above response, R Studio was installed successfully and you are ready to submit more complicated statements.

Also, you've just submitted your very first R code! Congratulations!

1.2.2 Workflow in the R Studio environment.

As mentioned it the previous chapter, for the first time you open R Studio you will see 3 windows:

- Console (left-hand side),
- Environment (upper right-hand side),
- Plots/packages/help window (lower right-hand side).

1.2.2 Workflow in the R Studio environment.

In addition to these 3 windows, it is very helpful to open a script that pops up as a 4th window in the upper left-hand side corner. In order to open a script window, go to the navigation panel at the top of your screen and click on the icon that looks like a white sheet of paper with a green "+" sign on it. When you get the drop down, select a new "script".

At this point you should have 4 windows in your environment.

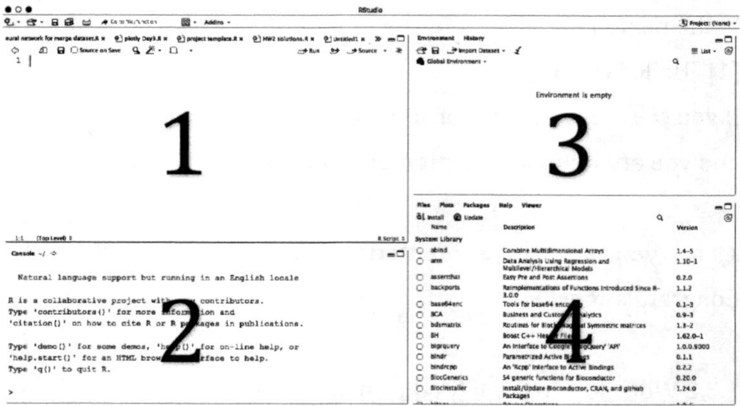

Picture 1.2.2.1: The R Studio environment [created by author]

Window number 1 is where you can browse all your scripts. It is possible to open more than one script if you need to reference different R programs. You will write your program in this window and submit it to the console using CTRL+ENTER. A good thing to point out at this point is that code is submitted line by line. Just

1.2.2 Workflow in the R Studio environment.

place your cursor on the row you want to submit and use CTRL+ENTER. In order to run multiple lines at a time, select the desired lines using your mouse and when all are highlighted, use CTRL+ENTER.

Window number 2 is called the console. This is where all the statements you submit from the script are executed. I refer to this window as a dialog box with R, where the compiler "talks" with the user about any errors or results. Besides printing errors and objects, you can submit code in the console. However, you cannot save any of your work in the console to reuse it in your next R session.
In addition to the console, R Studio allows you to use a terminal in the same, lower left-hand side corner of your screen, just select the proper tab at the top of the 2nd window.

Window number 3 is called the environment. This is where you will see all objects created and saved in your R script. To create an object in your environment, you need to assign a name using the following template:

```
my_name <- my_object
```

The above template has three elements:

- my_name – the name of the object, it will appear in the environment.
- <- the equal sign in R – this assigns the name to the object
- my_object – an object created using a function or by transforming an existing object

You can also use the "Import data" button to upload datasets in different formats. This feature is called the Data Import Wizard (DIW). When using the DIW, there will be a window in the bottom right hand corner of the screen where you can copy the code and reuse it in the future. What is more, as you progress in R coding you will discover the use of local and global environments.

Window number 4 has a lot of different applications. This window allows the user to:
- View and browse plots and graphs,
- Update, load, and install packages/libraries,
- Use the "help" feature to find information about libraries and functions.

1.3 Exercises

1. In the console, submit "Hi, my name is John". What is the result? What was the impact on the other windows?

2. In a new script, submit using CTRL+ENTER:

```
"Hi, my name is Judy"
```

What is the result of this code? Were any of the other windows impacted?

3. Submit from the script using CTRL+ENTER:

```
?sd
```

What did you get in return? Can you tell what "sd" is and how to run it?

4. Submit from the script using CTRL+ENTER:

```
?sum
```

What did you get in return? Can you tell what "sum" is and how to run it?

5. Submit from the script using CTRL+ENTER:

```
?plot
```

Based on the help document, are the data inputs understandable? What options can we select for the plot?

6. Create an object in your environment called "my_object" with the following content: "Hello master ". What data type was the new object assigned to?

7. Run the following:

```
testing_obj <- sd(c(1,2,3,4,5))
```

What was saved in the environment? How does this differ from the previous exercise?

8. Download the dataset from (copy and paste the link to your browser, the file will download automatically) http://mba.tuck.dartmouth.edu/pages/faculty/ken.french/ftp/ F-F_Research_Data_Factors_CSV.zip

and import the dataset using the DIW.

a) Copy the code from the DIW and paste it to your script.

b) Save your script on your local drive.

9. Open the file you downloaded to your local drive in #8 and delete the first column. Import the modified file using the script saved in 8.b

2. Data objects

2.1 Vectors, matrices, and data frames

Every object that you create in R is based on a vector. Even more complex objects are based on multiple vectors.

A vector is a sequence of numbers or characters in which order matters. It's best to imagine a simple vector of 2 elements. Let's consider a vector that describes a movement on a map. The first element (number) will describe how far an object moved in longitudinal distance. The second element (number) will tell us how far an object moved in the latitudinal distance. When we put these two numbers together, we get a vector describing how far the object moved in these two dimensions.

There are a few ways to create a vector (the following vectors create numeric vectors with integers):

```
X1 <- c(1,2,3)
X2 <- rep(c(1,2), each=4)
X3 <- seq( from=1, to=3, by=1)
```

The first approach (X1) is the most common, in which you can design any vector. Vector X1 has 3 elements: 1, 2, and 3. The second method (X2) is used when we have a repetition of elements and the last method works best if there is linear pattern.

A vector can be classified by the type of data it contains. Some of the basic vector types are (with examples):

- Numeric (listed in the code snippet above),
- Character - c("January", "February", "March"),
- Date – c("2018-5-5", "2018-5-6"),
- Factor – c("yes", "yes", "yes", "no", "no") but it translates to c(1,1,1,0,0),
- Logical – c("True", "False").

Stacking multiple vectors of the same type (numeric) will give us a matrix. A matrix will look like this:

$$\begin{pmatrix} 1 & 2 & 3 \\ 4 & 5 & 6 \\ 7 & 8 & 9 \end{pmatrix}$$

This matrix would have [3,3] dimensions. The first number is the count of rows and the second number is the count of columns. In this case we have 3 rows in 3 columns, thus the matrix dimensions are [3,3].

Here's a template:

> my_object[row_index , column_index]

This template will be very useful in the next chapter, when we cover sub-setting matrixes and data frames. In order to create a new matrix use the matrix() function. The inputs are your numeric vectors.

A data frame looks very similar to a matrix. However, we need to mention that data frames have column and row names. What is more, all the data in one column needs to be of the same type.

```
> print(kyphosis)
   Kyphosis Age Number Start
1    absent  71      3     5
2    absent 158      3    14
3   present 128      4     5
4    absent   2      5     1
5    absent   1      4    15
6    absent   1      2    16
7    absent  61      2    17
8    absent  37      3    16
9    absent 113      2    16
10  present  59      6    12
```

This console screen shot presents the first 10 rows of the kyphosis dataset. Notice, that each column has only one data type. The Kyphosis column is a factor and all other columns are numeric. In this case, the row names are indexed from 1 to 10.

When referencing the columns, we use the data set name followed by the dollar sign. In this case it will be:

- kyphosis$Age,
- kyphosis$Number,
- kyphosis$Start,
- kyphosis$Kyphosis.

Please be careful with the Kyphosis column name, as the data set is called "kyphosis" (lower case K) and the column is called "Kyphosis" (upper case K). R is case sensitive.

The template for referencing a column is as follows:

```
dataset_name$column_name
```

Just like matrixes, data frames can be also referenced using indexes using template.

It is worth mentioning that there are other objects in R, such as user defined functions, lists, values, etc. Some libraries create library specific objects (xtm or xts for time series).

2.2 Testing and changing the type of objects

In the previous chapter, we've discovered different vector types. These types are assigned to vectors based on the type of data that they store.

The most powerful function to test an object (including a vector) for its type is:

```
typeof(object_name)
```

The user can also test an object for a certain type using a family of functions:

```
>is._type_(object_name)
```

Here are a few examples:

```
is.character(object_name)
is.numeric(object_name)
is.logical(object_name)
is.data.frame(object_name)
is.character(object_name)
```

For data frames and long vectors, there are a few functions that help the user understand the data. Most of these functions will give basic summary statistics and the type of data stored in the object:

```
summary(object_name)
```

```
head(object_name)
str(object_name)
```

There are also many functions to change the type of data in an object. To convert data types use this family of functions:

```
as._type_(object_name)
```

Here are a few examples:

```
as.character(object_name)
as.numeric(object_name)
as.logical(object_name)
as.data.frame(object_name)
as.character(object_name)
```

2.3 Writing comments in your script

Before we cover sub-setting the objects, it is important to understand how to write comments and how they work in R. Comments are extremely important for a few reasons. They create breaks in your code, so that you can make it more readable, you can explain what your code is doing, or you can comment out unused code for future reference without deleting it.

A comment starts with a "#". When this special character is present, R skips further execution for a particular line.

When "#" is the first character in a given line, the entire line is skipped by the R compiler.

```
# this will not be executed
```

However, if the "#" is after some code in the same line, the initial code will be executed:

```
my_object <- sd(1,2,3) # only the object will be executed
```

Remember to put as many comments in your code as possible. It'll make your life easier in the future.

It is extremely important to use comments when coding more advanced programs with loops or user defined functions. These structures can be lengthy and need to be opened with (or { and closed with) or }, depending on the structure. When there is more than a few lines of code inside these structures, it becomes almost impossible to find the closing) or }. A good practice is to write comments that will tell the reader which loop or function is being opened or closed.

```
for( i in 1:100){        # opening the i-loop
    ...

    ...

    ...

        }            #closing the i-loop
```

2.4 Sub-setting objects using names and indexes

We've mentioned in the previous chapter that vectors are objects with elements for which order matters. This order is called indexing. Indexes start from 1 and are sequenced by1.

```
my_vector <- c(2008, 2009, 2010, 2011)
indexes <- c(1,2,3,4) #or seq(from=1, to=4, by=1)
```

Sub-setting vectors can happen index by index or for a range of indexes.

Index by index (referencing data in my_vector from the previous code snippet):

```
my_vector[1]
```

This will result in a one element vector with a value of 2008.
Range of indexes:

```
my_vector[1:3]
```

This will result in a vector with values of 2008, 2009, 2010.

Matrixes and data frames can be subset the same way. However, it is different from sub-setting vectors in the fact that they have two dimensions. Sub-setting needs to be performed on both, rows and columns:

```
new_df[row_index, column_index]
```

If one of the two indexes are empty, than all the elements pass on to the new object.

```
new_df[1:30, ] #all columns pass on to new object
```

As mentioned in chapter 2.1, data frames are objects with more attributes. The most important attribute of a data frame is its column names. We can subset one column using indexing (only one dimension as it becomes a vector):

```
mydata$mycolumn[1:30] # this will give us the first 30
# elements of the column
```

If you want to create a new data frame with just a few columns, you can specify a vector with column names in the column index. Use the following template if you want to copy the "Date" and "Names" columns only:

```
my_new_df <- my_old_df[ ,c("Date", "Names")]
```

In order to subset a data frame by putting a filter on values in a given column, use the which() function:

```
sub_df <- mydf[which(mydf$Age>10), ]
```

In the example above, we have selected all the rows(observations) that have age above 10. The column index is empty, which means that all columns are transferred to the new data frame.

The which() function is also great when it comes to cleaning up any observation that has missing values in a given column(variable). It will need to be combined with the is.na() function:

```
sub_df <- mydf[-which(is.na(mydf$Age)),    c("Age", "Number")]
```

The which statement pulls all the observations from the Age column (mydf$Age) that are NAs, in other words, have missing values. However, the main purpose was to eliminate them and this is why we used the minus sign in front of which(). The negative sign gave the remaining indexes, that were not part of the which(is.na()) statement.

2.5 Importing and exporting data sets

You can import data using the Data Import Wizard that is available from the environment window. Another way to import a dataset would be to use one of the functions from the readr package. A readr cheat sheet is available in the Appendix.

Before you write the function to import a dataset, it is highly recommended to convert the data to a text format .csv or an Excel format .xls (.xlsx works too).

The most commonly used template looks like this:

```
library(readr)
mydf <- read_csv("file.csv")
```

The *file.csv* argument has to be replaced with the file's directory. WARNING! You need to replace a forward slash "/" with a backslash "\" in the path as R requires backslashes when referencing a directory.

There is a similar function to write a .csv file containing an R data frame.

```
library(readr)
write_csv(x, "path.csv")
```

Were x is the data frame from the R environment and path.csv is the local directory where you want to write the file.

For more information on how to import or export data, go to the Appendix chapter and look for the "readr" cheat sheet.

2.6 Cleaning and sub-setting your data

After importing the data, open it using one of the following functions:

```
View(data_name)
print(data_name)
```

Do you understand all the variables (columns)? Do you need to go back to your metadata to learn more about your dataset? Are all the imported variables important?

Once you have a good understanding of the data, you can start sub-setting it. All the templates from the previous chapter are very helpful.

```
my_new_df <- my_old_df[ ,c("Date", "Names")]
sub_df <- mydf[which(mydf$Age>10), ]
sub_df1<-  mydf[-which(is.na(mydf$Age)),   c("Age", "Number")]
```

There is also a wrapper function, easier to understand. We can rewrite the sub_df data frame as follows:

```
sub_df <- subset(mydf, Age>10)
```

What is more, you might come across data that has a lot of missing values. In order to eliminate missing values from one column, you can use the **–which(is.na())** listed above. If there are multiple variables with missing values and you want to remove all observations that have at least one missing value, use the following:

```
clean <- na.omit(mydf)
```

2.7 Exercises

NOTE: Exercises marked with ** are advanced and require more time and research to solve.

1. Create vectors that have the following elements (do NOT use the c() function):

x1 = {10, 20, 30, 40, 50, 60, 70, 80, 90}

x2 = {60, 45, 30, 15, 0, -15}

x3 = {10, 100, 1000, 10000}

x4 = {243, 81, 9, 3}

2. Create the following character vector and change it to numeric:

y = {"1+2", "0101", "5*5"}

3. Import the kyphosis dataset using the library(rpart) and using the summary() function, give IQR (Inter Quartile Ranges) for the columns.

a) Change the $Kyphosis column to a numeric variable (it will end up being binary)

b) Subset the dataset for the Age and Number columns. Create a new object called "my_new_kyphosis".

4. For exercises 1-3 write comments with an explaination of the logic you've used to create the objects.

5. Create a new vector with the following elements (use indexing):

- 1st element of vector x1 from exercise 1,
- 2nd element of vector x1 from exercise 1,
- 5th element of vector x2 from exercise 1,
- 1st element of vector x1 from exercise 1,
- 3rd element of vector x4 from exercise 2.

a) Subset the new vector for any elements that are greater or equal to 20.

6. Subset the my_new_kyphosis dataset, which was created in exercise 3, so that the result has all the observations with Age:

a) less than 80. Use the which() function

b) equal to 1. Use the which function. (hint: use "==" to compare)

c) export the data from letter "a" to your local drive.

7. Create the following matrix and get the diagonal using the sub-indexing frameworks provided in chapter 2.4:

$$\begin{pmatrix} 10 & 11 & 9 & 15 & 19 \\ 52 & 19 & 7 & 10 & 22 \\ 28 & 40 & 6 & 99 & 33 \\ 35 & 26 & 5 & 87 & 91 \\ 0 & 12 & 16 & 81 & 200 \end{pmatrix}$$

8. Import the iris dataset (it's a build in R dataset).

a) Create an object so that the dataset goes to your environment,

b) Subset the entier dataset so that all the observations have Sepal Length greater than 5,

c) What is the difference between the variable distributions (for all variables) of the entire iris dataset and the subset from 8b.

9** Save a SAS dataset using the following data step:

>libname new "...*your C://Desktop.... Path*";

>data new.mysasdata ;

>input ID $ WEIGHT SIZE;

>dataline;

>101 150 3

>102 125 2

>105 210 6

>99 99 5

>110 199 5

> ;

>run;

a) Import the SAS dataset using a function from the READR cheat sheet.

b) What type are the columns?

c) Are the column data types different from the data types in SAS?

10**. Using the Fama French data from Exercise 8, Chapter 1, clean up all records that are missing. Make sure to exclude any missing values in all of the columns. Export your results to your local drive.

11**. Find AQR factors from the www.images.aqr.com/Insights/Datasets website and import the data directly from the url using the download.file() function. Is your data clean? If needed, subset and remove empty values from your dataset.

3. Functions

When trying to solve any given problem or challenge using R, you will end up trying to find a function that solves your problem. Fortunately, any challenge that you might be facing was most likely encountered by someone else in the past and described or solved by other R community members. Since R is an open source project, people create functions and post them in packages on the CRAN. This is how you can solve your problem without reinventing the wheel. At this point you might be wondering how are you supposed to know which function to use for your problem. In this case a google search might be your best option.

3.1 Packages / libraries – installation and usage

Packages ("libraries" is a synonym) are designed in a way to host multiple functions for a given subject. For example, if you needed to create multilayer plots (any type), you would call the ggplot2 package, or if you needed to build a decision tree, you would call the rpart package. Here's a list of some of the most popular packages and the subject that they cover:

- ggplot2 – plotting,
- plyr – dataframe manipulation

- stringr – character variable manipulation
- colorspace – defining colors
- reshape2 – data manipulation
- RColorBrewer – creating color palettes

All these packages can be downloaded from the CRAN using the

```
install.packages("name_of_package")
```

Other packages, that were developed recently, are located on GitHub. You will need to know the link in order to download these packages.

The installation process takes the file from CRAN or GitHub and installs it on your local drive, in a folder that R has created to store all packages. The install.packages("") function needs to be submitted only once. Next time, when you open R, all you will need to do is call the library without having to downloaded it again.

A package/library is called using:

```
library(name_of_library)
```

You will need to call a library each time you open a new R session. To make a script more structured, it is recommended to list out all the libraries, that the code requires, in the header of the script. A script header may look like the example below:

```
############################
#Created by XYZ on MM/DD/YYYY
#Title of the script
############################
library(ggplot2)
library(rprat)
library(princomp)
```

3.2 Functions from libraries

As mentioned in the chapter 3.1, libraries combine multiple functions that cover the same subject. You can find information on each function in a library from its documentation. These documents are available online and can be found from the google search engine using key words such as *"library_name documentation pdf"*. The description section of the document will tell us what the topic (subject) of all the functions is. The "R topic documented" section will give us a list of all functions that are in the rpart library. Each function will be described in the second part of the pdf document. The "Format" sections will list all the function inputs. It is very important to understand what objects and input formats the function needs to run properly.

Attached is a document that lists and describes all rpart library functions.

Package 'rpart'

February 23, 2018

Priority recommended

Version 4.1-13

Date 2018-02-23

Description Recursive partitioning for classification,
regression and survival trees. An implementation of most of the
functionality of the 1984 book by Breiman, Friedman, Olshen and Stone.

Title Recursive Partitioning and Regression Trees

Depends R (>= 2.15.0), graphics, stats, grDevices

Suggests survival

License GPL-2 | GPL-3

LazyData yes

ByteCompile yes

NeedsCompilation yes

Author Terry Therneau [aut],
Beth Atkinson [aut, cre],
Brian Ripley [trl] (producer of the initial R port, maintainer
1999-2017)

Maintainer Beth Atkinson <atkinson@mayo.edu>

Repository CRAN

Date/Publication 2018-02-23 05:45:50 UTC

R topics documented:

1

`car.test.frame`   *Automobile Data from 'Consumer Reports' 1990*

Description

The `car.test.frame` data frame has 60 rows and 8 columns, giving data on makes of cars taken from the April, 1990 issue of *Consumer Reports*. This is part of a larger dataset, some columns of which are given in `cu.summary`.

Usage

`car.test.frame`

Format

This data frame contains the following columns:

`Price` a numeric vector giving the list price in US dollars of a standard model

`Country` of origin, a factor with levels 'France', 'Germany', 'Japan' , 'Japan/USA', 'Kcrea', 'Mexico', 'Sweden' and 'USA'

`Reliability` a numeric vector coded 1 to 5.

`Mileage` fuel consumption miles per US gallon, as tested.

`Type` a factor with levels `Compact Large Medium Small Sporty Van`

`Weight` kerb weight in pounds.

`Disp.` the engine capacity (displacement) in litres.

`HP` the net horsepower of the vehicle.

car90   3

Source

Consumer Reports, April, 1990, pp. 235–288 quoted in

John M. Chambers and Trevor J. Hastie eds. (1992) *Statistical Models in S*, Wadsworth and Brooks/Cole, Pacific Grove, CA, pp. 46–47.

See Also

`car90`, `cu.summary`

Examples

```
z.auto <- rpart(Mileage ~ Weight, car.test.frame)
summary(z.auto)
```

---

car90   *Automobile Data from 'Consumer Reports' 1990*

Description

Data on 111 cars, taken from pages 235–255, 281–285 and 287–288 of the April 1990 *Consumer Reports* Magazine.

Usage

```
data(car90)
```

Format

The data frame contains the following columns

Country a factor giving the country in which the car was manufactured

Disp engine displacement in cubic inches

Disp2 engine displacement in liters

Eng.Rev engine revolutions per mile, or engine speed at 60 mph

Front.Hd distance between the car's head-liner and the head of a 5 ft. 9 in. front seat passenger, in inches, as measured by CU

Frt.Leg.Room maximum front leg room, in inches, as measured by CU

Frt.Shld front shoulder room, in inches, as measured by CU

Gear.Ratio the overall gear ratio, high gear, for manual transmission

Gear2 the overall gear ratio, high gear, for automatic transmission

HP net horsepower

HP.revs the red line—the maximum safe engine speed in rpm

Height height of car, in inches, as supplied by manufacturer

Length overall length, in inches, as supplied by manufacturer

Picture 3.2.1 Documentation for the rpart library. [source: R-CRAN]

Once we know which function we want to use, we can ask R to give us some help using the following template:

> ?*function_name*

For example, to get help on the rpart() function, we would submit the following (need to have the rpart package installed first):

> ?rpart

This will bring up the help document in the 4th window (lower right-hand corner) in our environment.

rpart {rpart}   R Documentation

Recursive Partitioning and Regression Trees

Description

Fit a rpart model

Usage

```
rpart(formula, data, weights, subset, na.action = na.rpart, method,
      model = FALSE, x = FALSE, y = TRUE, parms, control, cost, ...)
```

Arguments

formula	a formula, with a response but no interaction terms. If this a a data frame, that is taken as the model frame (see model.frame).
data	an optional data frame in which to interpret the variables named in the formula.
weights	optional case weights.
subset	optional expression saying that only a subset of the rows of the data should be used in the fit.

Picture 3.2.2 Usage and arguments of the rpart function. [source: R-CRAN]

In the upper left corner, the help document will tell us the name of the library to which this function belongs. In this case it is library(rpart).

The "Usage" section will have the function template. This is the most important section of the help document because it tells the user how the inputs are named and what inputs the function needs.

The "Arguments" section will give some detail on each function input. Please keep an eye on the data types that are required and how the input object is supposed to be designed.

Many times, this document will provide a few examples on the last page for the user to reference.

3.3 User defined functions

When trying to automate repetitive tasks, R allows to create user defined functions. A user created function must be saved to the environment with a custom name to be able to recall it later in the script. Here's the template:

```
function_name <- function( x , y, z) {
                temp_object1 <- ........
                temp_object2 <- ........
                temp_object3 <- ........
                return(temp_object3)
                }#this closes the function
```

The above script has a few elements:

- *function_name* – this is the name of the function that will be used to recall it later in the script

- **function** – this is the function used to create a user defined function
- (x, y, z) – these are the function parameters a.k.a. inputs
- {...} - these French braces open and close the body of the function – this is where all the operations are saved
- **return(...)** – specifies which object is to be returned when the user defined function is called – usually a data frame, matrix, or vector – the return() statement is at the end of the body, before the closing braces

Calling the user defined function happens the same way as calling a function from a CRAN package. Using the above example, the call would look like this:

```
function_name(x=my_x, y=my_y, z=my_z)
```

This will return the temp_object3 that is produced using the inputs that were specified in the function call.

One of the main reasons for using a user definied function is to avoid copy pasting the same code multiple times in one script when only a few objects or variables change each time. Instead, you can use a few function calls with different parameters.

```
output1 <- function_name(x=my_x1, y=my_y1, z=my_z)
output2 <- function_name(x=my_x2, y=my_y2, z=my_z)
...
```

```
output10   <-   function_name(x=my_x10,   y=my_y10,
z=my_z)
```

3.4 Exercises

1. Install all most common packages on your local machine. You can find a list of packages in chapter 3.1

2. Create your own script header. Make sure you include all information about yourself so that it serves as a business card as well. Make sure it doesn't execute with the other R code using the "comment" option.

3. Find the best library to build a neural network (type: perceptron).
a) Install the library,
b) Read the library documentation from CRAN,
c) Get the R help document for the function that trains the model (hint: fist, find the function from the library document, secondly, use the "?" option to get help on the function)

4.Repeat exercise 3a,b,c for a library that allows you import financial instrument pricing data. For letter C, find the function that allows to import time series of prices for a given ticker.

5. Get pricing data for the following tickers using the function from 4:

a) SPY (the ETF that represents the market)

b) S

c) FB

d) DB

e) WFC

Save these in separate data frames in your environment.

6. Using the Box.test function (find the documentation to understand the function) test each of these time series datasets if they are stationary or non-stationary. (do you need to transform the data?)

a) Which of these stocks can be modeled using ARMA and which using ARCH or GARCH?

c) Build the ARMA or ARCH or GARCH models for each of these stocks.

7.Create a user defined function named *studentfunction* that transposes a numeric matrix (columns become rows) and subsets the matrix in a way so that only the first 5 rows remain in the dataset.

a) Use the *studentfunction* function to transform the matrix created in Exercise 7 from chapter 2.

b) Use the *studentfunction* function to transform the matrix that was given as an example in chapter 2.1

8.Create a user defined function named *transformmatrix* that takes the diagonal of a matrix and calculates a vector with two elements. Element one is the mean of the diagonal and element two is the median.

a) Use the *transformmatrix* function to transform the matrix created in Exercise 7 from chapter 2.

b) Use the *transformmatrix* function to transform the matrix that was given as an example in chapter 2.1

9**. Create a user defined function that uses a quandl package to import zero coupon bond interest rates (the function inputs are the "from" and "to" dates and "N") and calculates N-day moving averages for the following maturities:

a) 3M

b) 1Y

c) 10Y

d) 30Y

Consider N = {25, 75, 250, 500} ; from={"07-01-2011", "01-30-2010" } ; to={"12-20-2018", most_currnet_date -1 }

4. Loops

Loops appear in almost any coding language. They are designed to run a certain chunk of code multiple times. Depending on the type of the loop, there might be conditions on how many times the loop runs.

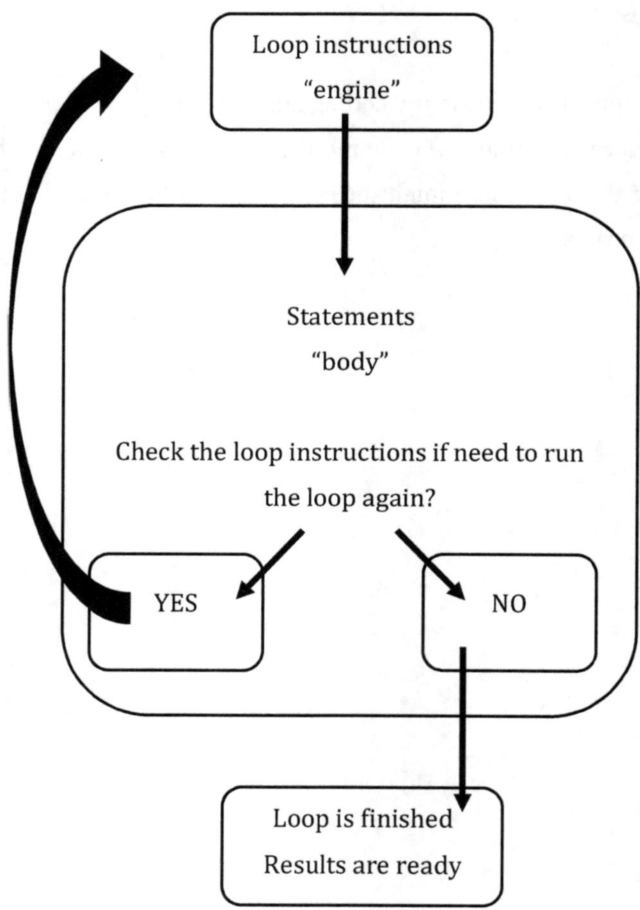

Graph 4.1: Generic loop design and data flow [designed by author].

4.1 The "FOR" loop

For loops run all the statements from the "body" for each element of a numeric vector. They are very powerful when it comes to manipulating and aggregating objects based on indexes. The template is as follows:

```
for( index_name in sequence) {
          statements
              }
```

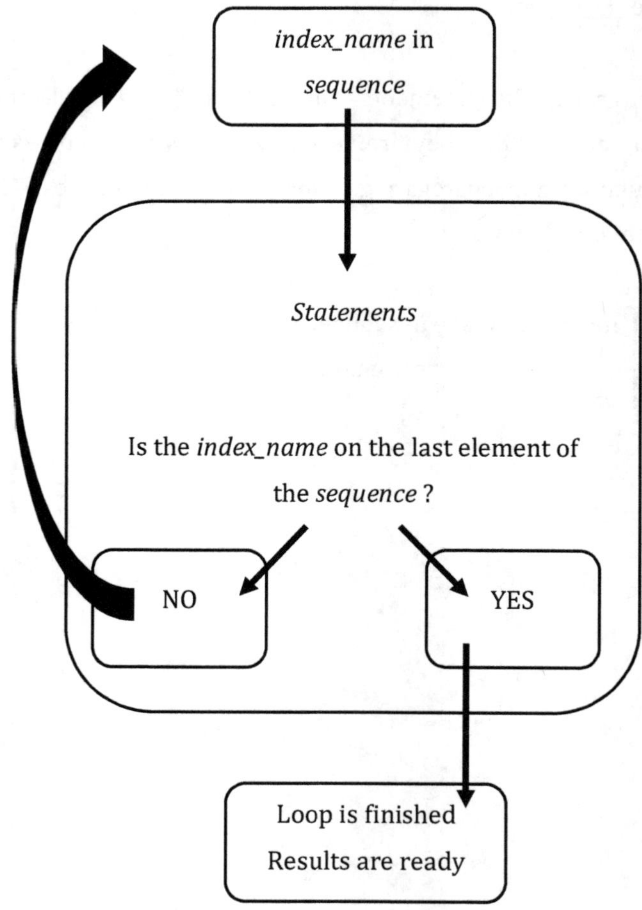

Graph 4.1.1: *For loop* design and data flow [designed by author].

There are a few elements in this code chunk that need to be adjusted based on the data objects:

- *Index_name* – in most cases, the index name is a lower case letter such as i, m, or n.
- *Sequence* – this should resolve to a numeric vector will elements that should be used for creating the index_name. A common solution is to write the following sequence with ":" such as 1:10. This would resolve to a vector (1, 2, 3, 4, 5, 6, 7, 8, 9, 10) and the loop would run 10 times.
- *statements* – (the "body") is what is being submitted for each element in the *sequence*. Any *index_name* reference will be substituted with a consecutive element from the *sequence.*

The first time the loop runs, the index name will take the first value from the sequence vector and substitute any reference in the statements. Each time the loop runs, the index name will take the next value from the sequence and put it in the statements. The loop stops when index name becomes the last element in sequence.

Let's consider the following loop:

```
for( i in 1:2) {
        print(i)
            }
```

This *for loop* will execute the following statements:

```
print(1)
print(2)
```

The first time the loop runs, the "i" will be substituted with 1. The second time the loop runs, the "i" will be substituted with 2. What is more, loops can be nested. For each run of the upper loop, the lower loop will run all the *sequence* elements.

```
for (n in 3:5) {                    #upper loop
        for( i in 1:2) {            #lower loop
                print(i+n)
                }                   #closing the i loop
        }                           #closing the n loop
```

This *for loop* will execute the following statements:

```
print(1+3)
print(2+3)
print(1+4)
print(2+4)
print(1+5)
print(2+5)
```

4.2 The "WHILE" loop

The while loop works in a similar way in which the *for loop* works. The only difference is that the while loop will stop executing when a condition is met.

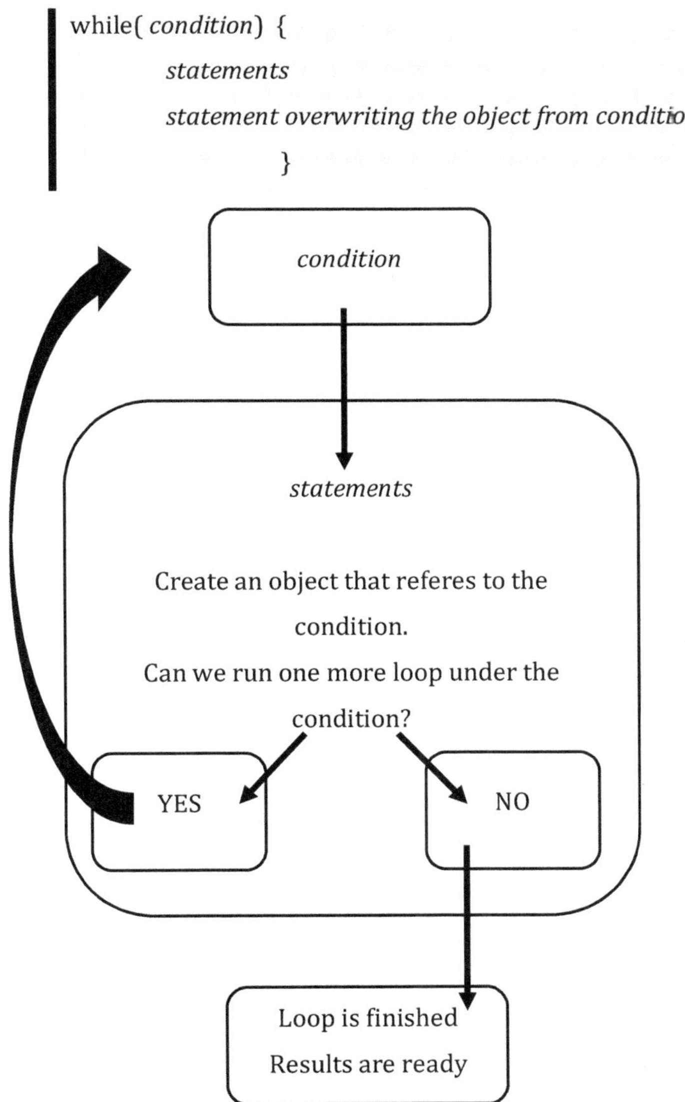

Graph 4.2.1: While loop design and data flow [designed by author].

The condition should include a numerical object that has a starting value that meets the condition.

What is more, the numerical object from the *condition* should be overwritten as one of the last steps in the *statements* section.

Let's consider the following loop:

```
i <- 0 #assigning the initial value for i
while( i <3) {
        i <- i+1
        print(i)
        }
```

This *for loop* will execute the following statements:

```
print(1)
print(2)
print(3)
```

4.3 Apply family function

Most *for loops* can be replaced by an "apply" function. The apply function takes a data object and performs a function on either the rows or columns (there are exceptions).

Here are all the functions from this family with their designated objects:

Function name	Data object
apply()	Columns or rows of a matrix
lapply()	Takes in a list and outputs a list
sapply()	Takes in a list and returns a vector
tapply()	Splits the input data based on a specified field
mapply()	Works the same way as sapply() but takes in multiple objects

Let's take a closer look at the apply() function as it is the most commonly used function from this family. When asking for help on this function (?apply), we get the following function description from CRAN:

Usage

```
apply(X, MARGIN, FUN, ...)
```

Arguments

X   an array, including a matrix.

MARGIN   a vector giving the subscripts which the function will be applied over. E.g., for a matrix 1 indicates rows, 2 indicates columns, c(1, 2) indicates rows and columns. Where X has named dimnames, it can be a character vector selecting dimension names.

FUN   the function to be applied: see 'Details'. In the case of functions like +, %*%, etc., the function name must be backquoted or quoted.

...   optional arguments to FUN.

Picture 4.3.1 Usage and arguments of the apply function. [source: R-CRAN]

The document presents the following template:

```
apply(x, margin, fun)
```

The first argument, x, stands for the data object, a data frame of a matrix. The second argument, margin, ask for a numeric input, 1 or 2.

1- the function is applied to rows

2- the function is applied to columns

The 3rd argument, called fun, is expecting a function name that will be used to aggregate the data. This could be a mean, sum, sd, etc.

4.4 Exercises

1. For the matrix created in Exercise 7 from chapter 4:

a) Calculate column medians using the apply() function.

b) Calculate row means using the apply() function.

2. For the matrix that was given as an example in chapter 2.1:

a) Calculate row medians using the apply() function.

b) Calculate column means using the apply() function.

3. Recreate the same processes from Exercise 1 and 2 using a for loop.

4. Using stock tickers from Exercise 5 from chapter 3:

a) Create a character vector with all tickers,

b) Create a loop to perform the same test as in Exercise 6 (chapter#3).

5. Create a while loop that will create a numerical vector with a sequence from 13 to 63.

6. Create a nested for loop (upper loop accounts for row indexes and lower loop accounts for column indexes) that creates a data frame with TRUE or FALSE inputs (logical data frame). The TRUE or FALSE will be an outcome of testing each cell from the kyphosis dataset for numeric type. (Hint: use is.numeric(kyphosis[upper_loop_index, lower_loop_index]))

7. Create the same logical data frame as in Exercise 6 using a while loop.

8. Create a list of matrixes using the following function:
```
new_list <- replicate(10, matrix(rnorm(4), 2, 2))
```
a) Using the appropriate function from chapter 4.3, get the median for each row for each matrix in the new_list.

9. For the iris dataset (no need to call a function, iris is part of the base R) create for loop that does the following to each observation:

a) changes the Species column from a character type to numeric. Assign 1 for setosa, 2 for virginica, and 3 for versicolor,

b) creates a new column that groups the Petal.Length into 3 groups: group#1 for Petal.Length from 0 to 2, group #2 from 2.01 to 4.5, and group #3 from 4.51 to 7.

10. Create a user defined function that can clean up almost any data frame using a loop. The function inputs are the dataset name and the column indexes that we want to clean up. An example of the function call might look like this:

```
function_name(x=mydata, col_idx=c(1,2,3))
```

The loop inside the function will take column indexes (from the call inputs) and remove observations with empty values.

Hint: inside the loop, use:

```
new_df <- x[-which(is.na(x[ ,col_idx[i]]))]
```

Test your function with any dataset found on the www.images.aqr.com/Insights/Datasets website.

11**. Create a for loop that simulates independent Geometric Brownian Motion Wt (~N(0,1)) for 5 hypothetical stocks.

$$\frac{dS_n}{S_n} = rdt + \sigma dW_t$$

The five stocks have the following annual growth rates and volatilities:

a) r=0.01 , sigma=0.1

b) r=0.02, sigma=0.12

c) r=0.03, sigma=0.14

d) r=0.04, sigma=0.16

e) r=0.05, sigma=0.18

Simulate the portfolio return for the first two years, if each stock is equally weighted in the portfolio and the allocation doesn't change over time.

12**. Create a for loop that creates a vector that creates elements using the following formula: $x_{i+1} = \sum_{i=0}^{i} x_i$.

Let $x_0 = 3$ and $x_1 = 5$. Use i=10 and i=20.

5. If statements

The main purpose of using *if statements* is to create an action based on a logical statement. It is very similar to the "if" clause, type 1 conditional, used in English grammar:

IF -> this statement is true -> this will happen (execute in R).

5.1 One possibility *if statement*

When there is only one condition that needs to be checked in the *if statement*, the "one possibility" *if statement* can be used.

```
if (condition){outcome}
```

The *condition* should give a logical (TRUE/FLASE) answer. Here are a few statement examples:

- if(mydf$Age[5] < 20){*outcome*}
- if(mydf$Name[1] == "Thomas"){*outcome*}
- if(my_constant == 10){*outcome*}

Each time the *condition* is TRUE, then the outcome is executed. The outcome can be any action such as creating a new object, or overwriting a value in a data frame.

The examples above cover only the TRUE response. However, we can easily define an action when the statement is FALSE.

> if (condition){outcome when TRUE}else{outcome when FALSE}

In this case, the *if statement* will always produce an output.

Even though there is only one condition checked in these *if statements,* they can have a form of multiple sub-conditions. The most common way to link sub-conditions is with the "OR" or "AND" statements:

> if (*condition1 || condition2*){*outcome*} # the || means OR
>
> if (*condition1 && condition2*){*outcome*} # the && means #AND

Example:

> if(mydf$Age[5]   <   20   &&   mydf$Name   ==
> "Tom"){*outcome*}

5.2 Nested *if statement*

When there is a need for multiple condition statements, a nested *if statement* has to be used.

> **if** (1st condition){outcome if 1st condition TRUE }
>
> **else if** (2nd condition){outcome if 2nd condition TURE}
>
> **else** {outcome if both are FALSE}

The above statement has a few elements:

- an opening **if** *statement* followed by the first condition
- multiple **else** **if** statements followed by different conditions
- an **else** statement that closes the entire string, it has the final outcome for a FALSE

All *condition* statements should give a logical (TRUE/FLASE) answer. Here are a few statement examples:

- if(mydf$Age[5] < 20){*outcome if TRUE*}else{outcome if FALSE}
- if(mydf$Name[1] == "Thomas"){*outcome if Thomas*} else if (mydf$Name[1] == "Mary"){*outcome if Mary*} else {*outcome if neither*}

The outcome can be any action such as creating a new object, or overwriting a value in a data frame.

Just like the one possibility *if statements*, the nested *if statements* can combine sub-conditions. The most common way to link sub-conditions is with the "OR" or "AND" statements:

```
if (condition1 || condition2){outcome} # the || means OR
if (condition1 && condition2){outcome} # the && means AND
```

5.3 Combining an *if statement* with a for loop

When using *if statements* on specific data points, we'll quickly realize that we need to test multiple data points in our data objects. For a vector, we might want to test all vector elements. For a data frame, the *if statement* can be applied for each cell in a given observation or variable. In these cases, we need to use the object's index(s) to write the *if statement*. The best way to run the "if" for each element is to put it in an indexing loop.

```
for ( i in 1:max_index){


if (1st condition with index i){outcome if 1st condition
TRUE } else if (2nd condition with index i){outcome if 2nd
condition TURE} else {outcome if both are FALSE}


}#closing the for loop
```

The example below uses the "x" data frame, which has two columns. The first column is numeric and has a few "1" (observations with value 1). For each observation with a value 1 in col1, we want to put a value 0 in col2.

```
for(i in 1:nrow(x)){

if(x$col1[i] == 1){x$col2[i] <- 0}else{x$col2[i] <- 1}

}#closing the for loop
```

5.4 Exercises

1.   Considering the $Age variable from the kyphosis dataset {library(rpart)} construct a one possibility *if statement* that:
a) Creates a new column named $group. For those observations that are older than 100 assigns a 1 and for those below or equal to 100, a 0 value.
b) Creates a separate vector with a TRUE value for all that are older than 80, and a FALSE value for all that are younger or at 80.
c) What is the type of the vector created in point b) . Can you convert it to numeric?

2. Considering the $Number variable from the kyphosis dataset {library(rpart)} construct a nested *if statement* that:
a) Replaces the current $Number variable with the following names: "up to 3" for values 1,2,or3, "more than 3 up to 5" for values 4, and 5, "more than 5" for any values greater than 5.
b) Creates a new column $mynewcol with the following:

- for $Kyphosis being "present" and $Number above 4 create a "bad" label in $mynewcol,
- for $Kyphosis being "absent" and $Number above 4 create a "good" label in $mynewcol,
- for any other combination, create a "unsure" label in $mynewcol.

3. Create a user defined function with an *if statement* that tests a vector from the function input. If the input vector is numeric, then the statement transforms the vector to character. If the input vector is character type, then the function returns the same character vector. The user defined function returns the new vector with all of its elements. Call the function using the following input vectors:

a) x1 <- c(1, 10, 5, 60, 80, 102, 101)

b) x2 <- c(8, 1, 3, 5, 6, 100, 99, 98)

c) x3 <- c("yes", "no", "yes", "no")

d) x4 <- c("0101", "1", "2", "22", "022")

e) x5 <- c("My", "favorite", "animal", "is", "a dog")

4. Using the user defined function from Exercise 10, chapter 4, put the *for loop* into an *if statement*. The *if statement* will allow the loop to run only if the first column (specified in the col_idx input) has more than 25% missing values. Use the following functions to get the percentage of missing values.

>nrow(x[which(is.na(x[,i]))])/length(x[,i])

5** Consider exercise 11 from chapter 4. As a last step, create an *if statement* that automatically excludes a stock from the final portfolio if it has lost value over the 2 years. If $\frac{dS_{2Years}}{S_0} < 0$ then exclude the stock and recalculate the weights for each remaining stock so that they are still equally weighted in the portfolio.

6. Estimation and optmization

There are many types of regressions. However, all of them have one thing in common. They take independent variable(s) and estimate a dependent variable. The distribution of the dependent variable will dictate the type of estimation and type of regression that needs to be used. This chapter will cover the two most common estimation/regression methods outlined in the table below.

Dependent variable distribution	Regression type	Estimation method
Continuous/Discrete	Linear	min(RSS)
Boolean/Binary	Logistic	max(log likelihood)

Table 6.1 Linear and logistic regression characteristics [created by author].

Please keep in mind that there are other estimation methods that will work better with different data e.g. time series.

6.1 Linear regression

Linear regression is a type of regression that fits a linear function to describe the relationship, called causation (not to be confused with correlation), between an independent variable(s) and the dependent variable. As stated in the prior chapter, the dependent variable should be continuous. Example of variables that can we regressed are: weight, height, length, size, salary, speed, age, etc.

Linear regression takes one or more independent variables X_1, X_2, X_3 ...., X_n (usually represented by X with a lower index) as inputs. On the other side of the equation is the dependent variable Y. The regression will assign "weights" to each and every independent variable. These weights are called "estimated coefficients" and will be denoted by $\widehat{\beta_1}$, $\widehat{\beta_2}$, $\widehat{\beta_3}$, ..., $\widehat{\beta_n}$.

For each set of beta, a new "estimated Y" will be calculated, denoted by $\hat{Y}$. The linear regression formula is as follows:

$$\hat{Y} = \widehat{\beta_0} + \widehat{\beta_1} *X_1 + \widehat{\beta_2} * X_2 + \widehat{\beta_3} *X_3 + \cdots + \widehat{\beta_n} * X_n$$

Where:

$\widehat{\beta_0}$- is the intercept

$\widehat{\beta_n}$- is the estimated n-th coefficient

$\hat{Y}$ - is the estimated dependent variable

There are different ways to estimate the best coefficients. The most popular method is called Ordinary Least Squares (OLS). The OLS minimizes the residual sum of squares (RSS) between the actual dependent response and the estimated value $\hat{Y}$.

In order to run a linear regression model in R, a data frame needs to be created with a few columns including the dependent and independent variables. The "dependent variable" column should be a continuous numeric variable. A sample data frame can look like the one below (weight is our dependent variable).

weight	age	cars	salary	sex
199.5	50	2	150000	Male
180.0	20	0	90000	Male
198.9	53	1	130000	Female
150.3	39	1	100000	Female

In R, the most popular function to run linear regression is the lm() function.

$$\mathrm{lm}(Y \sim X1+X2+X3+...+Xn\,,\,data=mydata)$$

lm {stats}   R Documentation

Fitting Linear Models

Description

lm is used to fit linear models. It can be used to carry out regression, single stratum analysis of variance and analysis of covariance (although aov may provide a more convenient interface for these).

Usage

```
lm(formula, data, subset, weights, na.action,
   method = "qr", model = TRUE, x = FALSE, y = FALSE, qr = TRUE,
   singular.ok = TRUE, contrasts = NULL, offset, ...)
```

Arguments

formula	an object of class "formula" (or one that can be coerced to that class): a symbolic description of the model to be fitted. The details of model specification are given under 'Details'.
data	an optional data frame, list or environment (or object coercible by as.data.frame to a data frame) containing the variables in the model. If not found in data, the variables are taken from environment(formula), typically the environment from which lm is called.
subset	an optional vector specifying a subset of observations to be used in the fitting process.
weights	an optional vector of weights to be used in the fitting process. Should be NULL or a numeric vector. If non-NULL, weighted least squares is used with weights weights (that is, minimizing sum(w*e^2)); otherwise ordinary least squares is used. See also 'Details',
na.action	a function which indicates what should happen when the data contain NAs. The default is set by the na.action setting of options, and is na.fail if that is unset. The 'factory-fresh' default is na.omit. Another possible value is NULL, no action. Value na.exclude can be useful.

Picture 6.1.1 Usage and arguments of the lm function. [source: R-CRAN]

Y and X1:Xn are column names and do not need to be written with the data frame name and $ sign because the data frame name is defined in the "data=*mydata*" argument.

The lm() function creates an object of class "lm" with a list of objects including all the model coefficients. Use the following code to get the coefficients:

```
my_coefficients <- mymodel$coefficients
```

It will also give the estimated "Y-hat" values:

```
my_estimates < mymodel$fitted.values
```

All the objects created by the lm() function are listed below.

Value

lm returns an object of class "lm" or for multiple responses of class c("mlm", "lm").

The functions summary and anova are used to obtain and print a summary and analysis of variance table of the results. The generic accessor functions coefficients, effects, fitted.values and residuals extract various useful features of the value returned by lm.

An object of class "lm" is a list containing at least the following components:

coefficients	a named vector of coefficients
residuals	the residuals, that is response minus fitted values.
fitted.values	the fitted mean values.
rank	the numeric rank of the fitted linear model.
weights	(only for weighted fits) the specified weights.
df.residual	the residual degrees of freedom.
call	the matched call.
terms	the terms object used.
contrasts	(only where relevant) the contrasts used.
xlevels	(only where relevant) a record of the levels of the factors used in fitting.
offset	the offset used (missing if none were used).
y	If requested, the response used.
x	If requested, the model matrix used.
model	if requested (the default), the model frame used.
na.action	(where relevant) information returned by model.frame on the special handling of NAs.

Picture 6.1.2 Values of the lm function. [source: R-CRAN]

In chapter2, we've mentioned the summary() function. It is also very powerful when trying to summarize a model.

```
summary(model_name)
```

The summary() function will print all the coefficients, errors, and significance tests for each independent variable. This output might be helpful when assessing the quality of the model and weather any of the variables should be excluded. The p-value should give a good indication of the statistical significance of an estimate. (We want to get p-values that are smaller than 0.05 or 0.1, if bigger, the coefficient is statistically insignificant and needs to be equaled to 0.)

The summary() function will also provide estimated values for coefficients β_n. The coefficient is easy to interpret because it describes the change in the dependent variable when the independent variable increases by one unit, ceteris paribus.

6.2 Testing for homoscedasticity.

Linear regression has a few assumptions, one of them being that the underlying data is homoscedastic. A good way of checking if the data is homoscedastic, is to create a scatter plot with the X variable on the X-axis and the Y variable on the Y-axis.

The chart below presents homoscedasticity and heteroscedasticity.

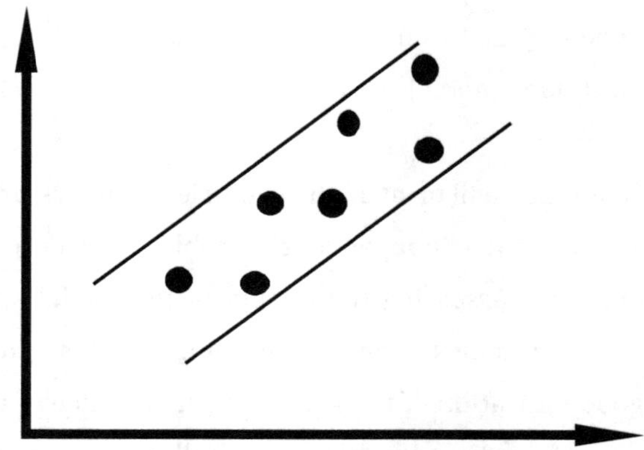

Chart 6.2.1 Homoscedasticity [created by author]

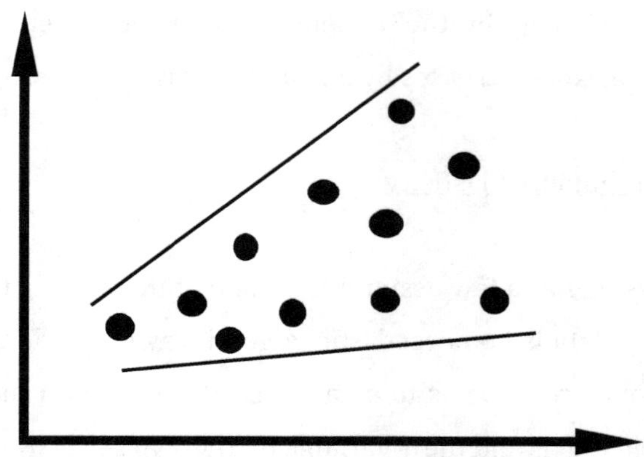

Chart 6.2.2 Heteroscedasticity [created by author]

Homoscedasticity is observed when the variance of Y is constant over all the values of X, chart 6.2.1. When the variance of Y depends on the value of X (increases or decreases when X changes) then we say we have heteroscedasticity.

Besides creating a scatterplot using the plot(x=*my_x_variable*, y=*my_y_variable*, type="p") function, we can run the Breush – Pagan test.

```
library(lmtest)
bptest(my_model_name)
```

If the p-value of this test is lower than the level of significance (lower than 0.05 or 0.1), you would reject the null hypothesis, and conclude that heteroscedasticity is present. The null hypothesis is that the data is homoscedastic (error variances are all equal). This is why we want bigger p-values to conclude homoscedasticity.

6.3 Logistic regression

Logistic regression is an estimation method that fits a sigmoid function between an independent variable and a binary variable. Binary variables are defined as variables with only two outcomes such as Yes/No, True/False, Male/Female, or 1/0. If the variable (vector in R language) is character or factor, than we should convert to a numeric type using any of the functions covered in previous chapters. After the conversion, the dependent variable should have only two values: 1 for the "success" outcome and 0 for the "failure" outcome.

The below chart shows a scatter plot (big black dots) representing our data. Notice, that the Y axis has only 2 values, 1 or 0.

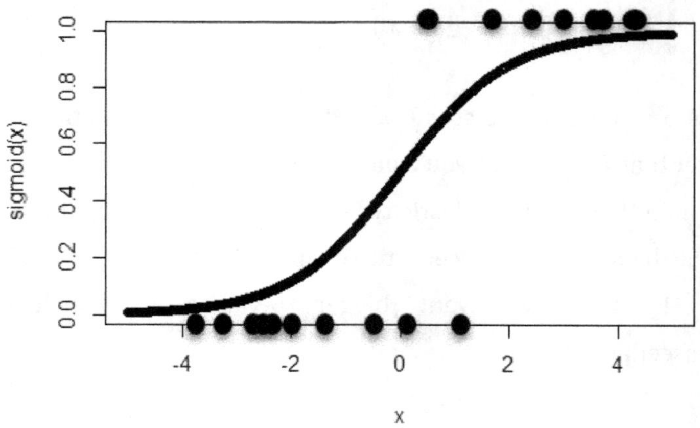

Graph 6.3.1: Fitted sigmoid function for logistic regression (from author's collection)

The coefficient(s) of the sigmoid function is(are) fitted using the maximum likelihood estimation method. This function is extremely useful because it outputs the probability of success, denoted as p(1), for any given value of X. With the sigmoid function, we can determine if an observation is more likely to be a 1 (if the probability is more than 0.5) or a 0 (if the probability is below 0.5).

As mentioned, the difference between a linear regression and logistic regression is that instead of estimating the value of the dependent variable, it will give the probability of 1, P(Y=1) for a binary variable (only 0 or 1 values). Here's the formula:

$$p(Y) = \frac{1}{1 + e^{-(\widehat{\beta_0} + \widehat{\beta_1}*X_1 + \cdots + \widehat{\beta_n}*X_n)}}$$

Where:

$\widehat{\beta_0}$ - is the intercept

$\widehat{\beta_n}$ - is the estimated n-th coefficient

p(Y) - is the probability of Y=1

The data frame needs to be compiled the same way as for the lm() function. A sample data frame can look like the one below.

purchase_decision	age	weight	salary	hair
1	50	190	150000	Brown
0	20	150	90000	Brown
1	53	210	130000	Black
0	39	200	100000	Black

However, the function for a logistic regression is called glm() , with the family="binomial" option.

```
glm(Y ~ X1+X2+X3+...+Xn , data=mydata, family="binomial")
```

Where Y and X1:Xn are column names and do not need to be written with the data frame name and $ sign because the data frame name is defined in the "data=*mydata*" argument.

The glm() function will give the following output:

Value

`glm` returns an object of class inheriting from `"glm"` which inherits from the class `"lm"`. See later in this section. If a non-standard `method` is used, the object will also inherit from the class (if any) returned by that function.

The function `summary` (i.e., `summary.glm`) can be used to obtain or print a summary of the results and the function `anova` (i.e., `anova.glm`) to produce an analysis of variance table.

The generic accessor functions `coefficients`, `effects`, `fitted.values` and `residuals` can be used to extract various useful features of the value returned by `glm`.

`weights` extracts a vector of weights, one for each case in the fit (after subsetting and `na.action`).

An object of class `"glm"` is a list containing at least the following components:

`coefficients`	a named vector of coefficients
`residuals`	the *working* residuals, that is the residuals in the final iteration of the IWLS fit. Since cases with zero weights are omitted, their working residuals are `NA`.
`fitted.values`	the fitted mean values, obtained by transforming the linear predictors by the inverse of the link function.
`rank`	the numeric rank of the fitted linear model.
`family`	the `family` object used.
`linear.predictors`	the linear fit on link scale.
`deviance`	up to a constant, minus twice the maximized log-likelihood. Where sensible, the constant is chosen so that a saturated model has deviance zero.
`aic`	A version of Akaike's *An Information Criterion*, minus twice the maximized log-likelihood plus twice the number of parameters, computed by the `aic` component of the family. For binomial and Poison families the dispersion is fixed at one and the number of parameters is the number of coefficients. For gaussian, Gamma and inverse gaussian families the dispersion is estimated from the residual deviance, and the number of parameters is the number of coefficients plus one. For a gaussian family the MLE of the dispersion is used so this is a valid value of AIC, but for Gamma and inverse gaussian families it is not. For families fitted by quasi-likelihood the value is `NA`.

Picture 6.3.1 Values of the glm function [source: R-CRAN].

Just like with the lm() function, the glm()creates an object of class "glm" with a list of objects including all the model coefficients. Use the following code to get the coefficients:

```
my_coefficients <- mymodel$coefficients
```

The coefficients need to be transformed in order to drive business insight. We need to take the exponent of the coefficient value to make it understandable.

```
insight <- exp(my_coeff)
```

This exponent value can be interpreted as the change in odds ratio assuming a one unit change in the independent variable, ceteris paribus. E.g. the coefficient is 0.5 and exp(0.5) = 1.64 and after subtracting 1 we get 0.64. This value represents the change in odds ratio. In this case that would be an increase in odds ratio by 64%.

When we want to compare a few models (maybe with different independent variables) we can use the Akaike Information Criterion. The lower the AIC the better. The AIC can be obtained by the following:

```
myAIC <- mymodel$aic
```

6.4 Predicting the dependent variable with a given model

What is more, the summary() function works just the same way as it does for the linear model.

```
summary(mymodel)
```

The summary() contains all the most important information about the logistic regression model.

6.4 Predicting the dependent variable with a given model

The models that we've build in the chapters 6.1 and 6.2 can be used to predict the dependent variable for new data. The new data needs to have all the independent variables that were used to build the model (the column names in the new data frame have to be the same as the column names in the data frame used to build the model). There can be multiple observations in the new data frame.

To predict the dependent variable for a linear model, use the predict() function:

```
my_new_dependent <- predict(model_name, my_data)
```

Where:

my_new_dependent -   will have all the predicted dependent outcomes, *model_name* - is the name of the model that we've designed in chapter 6.1,

my_data - is the name of the new data frame.

The function has one additional input when we want to predict the probability for new data using our logistic regression model:

```
new_prob        <-    predict(model_name,    my_data,
type="response")
```

The **type="response"** option will tell the predict() function that we need the true probability of 1, P(Y=1). If the new data frame, *my_data,* has more than one observation, the predict() function will output a vector of probabilities for each observation and save it in the "new_prob" object.

6.5 Non-parametric estimation using smoothing splines **

Not all data can be estimated using a linear regression especially when the relationship is non-linear. In this case, the best option would be to fit a n-th degree polynomial.
What is more, the relationship might change over time (usually X-axis as the predictor variable). This would mean that one polynomial cannot describe the entire time horizon.

6.5 Non-parametric estimation using smoothing splines **

With such a problem, using a smooth spline would be the best option.

Splines work in such a way that they divide the time horizon (or other predictor variable) into smaller frames using knots. The curves between the knots can be estimated using different polynomials. This is why mathematicians use the term "piecewise polynomials" for splines.

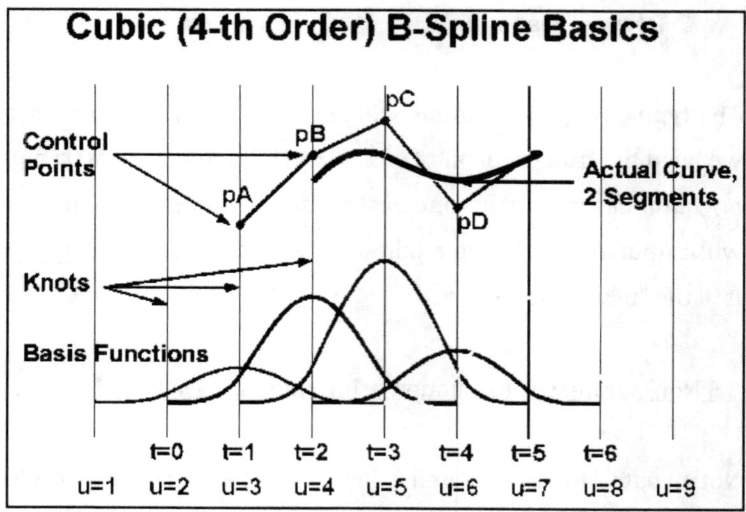

Graph 6.4.1: Cubic spline framework [Retrieved on 8/22/2018 from: https://people.eecs.berkeley.edu/~sequin/CS284].

R has a function that will optimize all the knots and find the best degree to fit the polynomials on the data.

6.5 Non-parametric estimation using smoothing splines **

> my_spline_model   <-   smooth.spline(x=*predictor*, y=*responses*, df=*number_df*)

Where:

x=*predictor* – is the predictor column in a data frame e.g. time[as an index)

y=*responses* – this is the Y variable in your data frame

df=*number_df* – the degree of polynomial that is being fitted, if not specified, the smooth.spline() will take the best fit.

Even though it's not required, it is a good practice to define the df in the smooth.spline() function. This way you can control the function and avoid overfitting. Many times, when the df option is omitted, the function will over fit the data.

The mathematical representation of the cubic spline function might be a bit confusing because the predictors are at higher degrees (n-degree polynomials). However, it is worth looking at it to have an understanding of what is being fitted on the data. Below is the function for cubic smooth spline regression:

$$E(Y|X) = \widehat{\beta_0} + \widehat{\beta_1} * X^1 + \widehat{\beta_2} * X^2 + \widehat{\beta_3} * X^3 + \widehat{\beta_4} * (X - a_1)^3 +$$
$$+ \widehat{\beta_5} * (X - a_2)^3 + \widehat{\beta_6} * (X - a_3)^3 + ... + \widehat{\beta_{k+3}} * (X - a_k)^3$$

6.6 Fitting function parameters

Sometimes, there is a function or equation that is not standard and needs to be implemented via a user defined function (chapter 3.3). These have usually more parameters that need to be estimated. What is more, parameters are usually noted using Greek letters: $\alpha, \beta, \gamma, \delta, \varepsilon, \theta$, etc.

In this situation, there has to be a user defined function:

```
my_function <- function(α, β, γ, δ, ε, θ) {
                temp_object1 <- .......
                temp_object2 <- .......
                temp_object3 <- .......
                return(temp_object3)
                }#this closes the function
```

And an optimization function that will optimize an objective considering the difference between the *temp_object3* and real data. Usually, the objective is to minimize the RSS (residual sum of squares) but you can use a MLE (maximum likelihood estimation) to fit any nonlinear relationships. As you can probably imagine by now, the temp_object3, which is returned by the function, and the real_data object need to be vectors(or matrixes) of the same dimensions/length. The optimization function comes from the library(minpack.lm) as has the following structure:

```
library(minpack.lm)
my_optimization      <-      nlsLM(real_data$Y      ~
my_function(α, β, γ), start = c(α = 1, β = 1, γ = 2),
lower = c(α = −5, β = −10, γ = −12),
upper = c(α = 20, β = 15, γ = 7)
)
```

The nlsLM() will return a list of optimized values for the $\alpha, \beta, and\ \gamma$ (function parameters). The "start" option defines the initial values at which the function will start the optimization, the "lower" will define a floor on each parameter, and the "upper" option will define a ceiling on the parameters.

Sometimes, there will be an error that says that the optimization hit a maximum number of allowed iteration. In this case, modifying the start, lower, or upper vectors might be helpful.

6.7 Exercises

1. Using the iris data frame (the data is part of base R and you can call it without installing any functions) build a linear regression that uses Sepal.Length as the dependent variable and the following as independent variables:

a) Sepal.Width

b) Petal.Length

c) Petal.Width

Build the 3 separate models with one independent variable per model. What can you say about the significance of the models and significance of the coefficients?

2.Using the kyphosis dataset (from library(rpart)) build linear regression models with the Age variable being the dependent variable and the following as independent variables:

a) Number,

b) Start.

Build separate models for each independent variables and one multivariate regression model for the two variable together.

Are any of the models statistically significant? Are any of the independent variables insignificant (alpha =0.1)?

For the multivariate model, which variable contributes the most to the independent variable (based on the value of the estimate)?

3.Using the iris dataset:

a) combine the Setosa and Versicolor into group "0" and label the Virginica to "1". Create a new variable called iris$Group with the 0 or 1 labels,

b) build a logistic regression model using any available data that will predict the observation being Virginica (value of 1 in Group variable),

c) calculate the probability of a new plant being a Virginica for the following parameters:

Sepal.Width =5

Petal.Length =10

Petal.Width =7

Sepal.Length=9

4.Using the kyphosis dataset:

a) convert the kyphosis$Kyphosis variable to numeric, assign a 1 to present and a 0 to absent,

b) build a logistic regression using all other variables and estimate the probability of the observation having a "present" hyphosis. What can you say about the coefficients? Are the significant?

c) calculate the probability of kyphosis being "present" for the following observation: Age=50, Start=10, Number=5.

5. Using all the single variable regressions from Exercise 1, test if the variable pairs are homoscedastic or heteroscedastic. Plot your findings. Using the plot(x=*my_x_variable*, y=*my_y_variable*, type="p") function. Use *my_data$variable_name* to define x and y variables in the function.

7. Using the Wage dataset from library(ILSR), use the smooth.spline() function to get a model for age being the independent variable and wage being the dependent variable? How good is your spline model?

8. Using the same function as in exercise 7, try to fit a cubic spline for age being the independent variable and logwage being the dependent variable (Wage dataset). Compare your results to the model from Exercise 7. Do they differ?

9**. Fit the following polynomial function:

$$\hat{Y} = \hat{\beta} + \hat{\theta}X^{\delta}$$

on the cars dataset from R. Use speed as your independent variable X and dist (distance) as your dependent variable Y. Get the estimated coefficients using the nlsLM() function.

10. Test the following regressions for heteroscedasticity:
- from exercise 1 in this chapter, using the Breuch-Pagan test,
- from exercise 2 in this chapter, using the Breuch-Pagan test,
- from exercise 7 in this chapter, using a scatter plot [plot() function with type="p"].

7. Data mining using SQL in R

7.1 The SQL template

The most basic SQL syntax includes 3 elements, the SELECT statement, the FROM statement, and the WHERE clause (the where clause is optional). The "SELECT statement" will list all the variable names that need to be exported from the table listed in the "FROM statement".

SELECT *variable_name1, variable_name2*
FROM *my_dataset*
WHERE *variable_name1 > value*

If we wanted to get all the Number values and Kyphosis status for those observations that have Age greater than 100 from the kyphosis dataset, library(rpart) , we would use the following SQL query:

SELECT a.Number, a.Kyphosis
FROM kyphosis a
WHERE a.Age > 100

The lower-case letter "a" is a reference letter for the kyphosis dataset. Each variable name with "a." in front of it, will be pulled from the "a" table. For queries that use only one dataset, the reference letter can be omitted, but needs to be used when joining multiple tables (see chapter 7.3).

What is more, SQL offers basic aggregation functions. The aggregation can be a SUM(*variable_name*), COUNT(*variable_name*), COUNT(DISTINCT *variable_name*), etc. For all of the aggregations, the SQL query needs to be extended with a GROUP BY clause. The GROUP BY will list the variables that are supposed to be combined at the aggregation level.

SELECT SUM(a.Number) AS Number_sum, a.Kyphosis
FROM kyphosis a
WHERE a.Age > 100
GROUP BY a.Kyphosis

A rule of thumb is to list all non-aggregated variables in the GROUP BY that are used in the SELECT statement.

Finally, SQL provides a very convenient and user intuitive way of creating labels and writing conditional statements. The CASE WHEN...... THEN ..... ELSE .... END is used very frequently and allows to perform similar operations as the "if statement" in R.

```
SELECT a.Kyphosis, CASE WHEN a.Number >20 THEN "older"
ELSE "younger" END AS new_label
FROM kyphosis a
```

The above SQL statement will create a new variable called new_label with "older" value when Number >20 and "younger" label when Number <=20.

The AS statement after a variable aggregation or conditional statement assigns a new variable name. In the example above, the conditional statement was labeled as a new variable called "new_label".

In the SELECT statement, each variable can be called separately, just like in the previous examples. However, all the variables can be called with the * , just like in the example below:

```
SELECT *
FROM kyphosis
```

This query will return all variables from the kyphosis dataset.

7.2 The sqldf() function

To run SQL in R, you need to install the SQLDF package and call the library(sqldf) in every new R session.

```
install.packages("sqldf")
library(sqldf)
```

After calling the library(sqldf), the sqldf() function will become available. It has the following structure:

```
new_df <- sqldf("
        SELECT *
        FROM kyphosis
        ") #closing the sqldf function
```

This function requires the SQL statement to be surrounded by "" so that it appears as a character. What is more, the dataset used in the sqldf() function must be a data frame. The function will not work on a matrix, vector, or list. It is recommended to use the as.data.frame() function on the object to make sure it is a pure data frame before using the sqldf().

In order to run the CASE WHEN example from the previous chapter, the following code has to be submitted:

```
new_data <- sqldf("
                SELECT a.Kyphosis,
        CASE WHEN a.Number >20 THEN "older"
        ELSE "younger"
        END AS new_label
                FROM kyphosis a
                ")
```

7.3 SQL data joins

When two or more data tables are in a relationship, they can be joined together. Both datasets will have one or more columns in common (that are the same). These columns are called primary key (for the table with distinct values in the common variable) and secondary key (for the table with multiple values in the common variable).

The relationship can be:

- one to one - one record from the first table corresponds to one record in the second table,
- one to many – one record from the first table corresponds to multiple records from the second table,
- many to one – multiple records from the first table correspond to one record from the second table,

- many to many – many records from the first table correspond to multiple records from the second table.

Once we know what the relationship looks like, we can determine which data join to use. What is more, the use of a particular data join will be determined by which data table is more important and if we want to exclude records from the less important data table.

There are multiple data joins that allow combining data in different ways. Here are to most common data joins:

- INNER JOIN – keeps only the records that find a match from both tables,
- FULL OUTER JOIN – keeps all the records from both datasets,
- LEFT JOIN – keeps all the records from the "left" table and drops records from the "right" table that weren't matched with the left table,
- RIGHT JOIN – keeps all the records from the "right" table and drops records from the "left" table that weren't matched with the right table.

The chart below shows what data is being passed to the outcome table in each join. The black area represents the data that is passed and the white area is the data that is dropped:

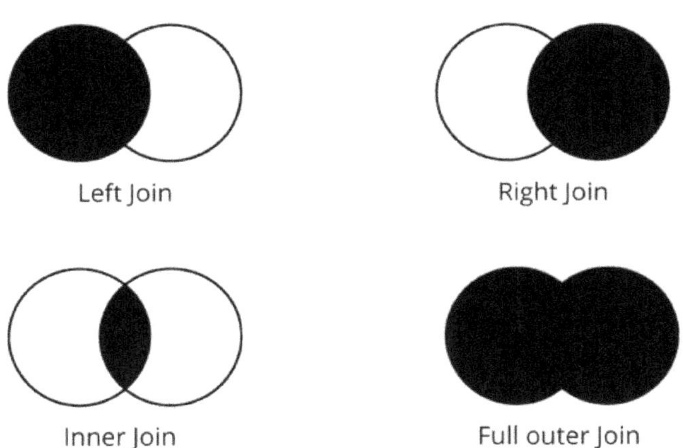

Graph 7.3.1 Data join types. [Retrieved on 8/22/2018 from:
https://www.quora.com/What-is-the-difference-between-joining-and-blending-in-Tableau]

Each join has its own template. The most common join templates are provided below.

SELECT *
FROM *table1* a
INNER JOIN *table2* b
ON a.*key_variable*=b.*key_variable*

```
SELECT *
FROM table1 a
LEFT JOIN table2 b
ON a.key_variable=b.key_variable


SELECT *
FROM table1 a
RIGTH JOIN table2 b
ON a.key_variable=b.key_variable


SELECT *
FROM table1 a
FULL OUTER JOIN table2 b
ON a.key_variable=b.key_variable
```

Each of the templates above has a JOIN statement and an ON statement. The JOIN statement will indicate the type of join and the table name that is being joined. The ON statement indicates which variables are supposed to be used to create the join. These ON statement variables will be the primary key and secondary key.

The library(dplyr) has an easy to use family of functions to perform joins:

```
library(dplyr)
my_join <- left_join(dataset1, dataset2, by = c('primary_key'))
my_join1 <- inner_join(dataset1, dataset2)
```

7.4 Exercises

1. Write a SQL query on the kyphosis dataset using the sqldf() function to get the following:

a) All the variables and all the observations,

b) Just the Number and Age variables and all the observations,

c) All the variables and only the observations that have Age greater than 50,

d) Just the Number and Age variables and only the observations that have Age smaller than 40,

e) Just the Kyphosis variable for all the observations with Number smaller than 5.

2. Write a SQL query on the iris dataset using the sqldf() function to get the following:

a) All the variables and all the observations,

b) Just the Sepal.Length and Sepal.Width variables and all the observations ,

c) All the variables and only the observations that have Sepal.Length greater than 4,

d) Just the Pedal.Length and Sepal.Width variables and only the observations that have Sepal.Length smaller than 4,

e) Just the Sepal.Length variable for all the observations with Sepal.Width smaller than 4.

3. Write a SQL query on the kyphosis dataset using the sqldf() function to get the specified aggregation for:

a) All the observations. Aggregate the data to get the sum of Age per each kyphosis outcome,

b) All the observations. Aggregate the data to get the arithmetic mean of Age per each kyphosis outcome,

c) Observations that have Age greater than 50. Aggregate the data to get the count of observations per each kyphosis outcome,

d) Observations that have Age smaller than 40. Aggregate the data to get the count of distinct Number values per each kyphosis outcome,

e) Observations with Number smaller than 5. Aggregate the data to get the count of distinct Number values per each kyphosis outcome.

4. Write a SQL query on the iris dataset using the sqldf() function to get the specified aggregation for:

a) All the observations. Aggregate the data to get the sum of Petal.Length per each Species group,

b) All the observations. Aggregate the data to get the arithmetic mean of Petal.Width per each Species group,

c) Observations that have Petal.Length greater than 3.5. Aggregate the data to get the count of observations per each Species group,

d) Observations that have Sepal.Width smaller than 3.4. Aggregate the data to get the count of distinct Sepal.Length values per each Species group,

e) Observations with Petal.Length smaller than 1.8. Aggregate the data to get the count of distinct Petal.Width values per each Species group.

5. Create the following joins for the specific datasets:

a) Inner join for airlines and airports from the library(nycflights13)

b) Left join for airlines and airports from the library(nycflights13)

c) Create the following datasets and perform a full outer join, left join, and right join:

Dataset A:

customer_id	first_name	last_name	age
1001	Paul	Smith	49
1002	John	Thomas	22
1003	Mary	Yip	15
1004	Thomas	Kurnicki	41
1005	Andrew	Rutky	32
1006	Jennifer	Yip	20

Dataset B:

customer_id	transaction_type	total_value
1001	1	55.99
1001	1	41.20
1001	2	69.01
1003	1	111.11
1002	1	19.00
1002	1	20.00
1006	2	28.40

d) Count how many observations are there in each of the new datasets created in a, b, and c.

6. Using the joins created in exercise 5.c calculate the following (use the sqldf() function for your calculation) :

a) Median of transaction_type for all transactions above $40,

b) Median of transcation_type for customers younger than 40,

c) Sum of total_value for all customers with truncation_type ecual to 2,

d) Count distinct cusomter_id,

e) Sum of total_value for each customer individually (group by customer),

f**) Frequency of transactions per customer,

g**) Frequency of transaction_types per customer.

8. Visualizations and interactive plots

8.1 The basic plot() function

Even though GGPLOT2 and PLOTLY have become extremely popular over the past few years, R has some native plotting capabilities that are faster to use and implement. The most basic R function for plotting data is the plot() function (no need to call a library, the plot() is a native R function).

```
plot(x, y, type="selected_type")
```

The plot() function can plot a few different types of charts. The *selected_type* can be:

- "p" for points,
- "l" for lines,
- "b" for both,
- "c" for the lines part alone of "b",
- "o" for both 'overplotted',
- "h" for 'histogram' like (or 'high-density') vertical lines.

The x from the function stands for the x-axis variable, whereas the y stands for the y-axis variable. These can be variables from a data frame and in this case they need to be specified in the data frame format mydf$variable_name .

Here's an example of a scatterplot using the plot() function:

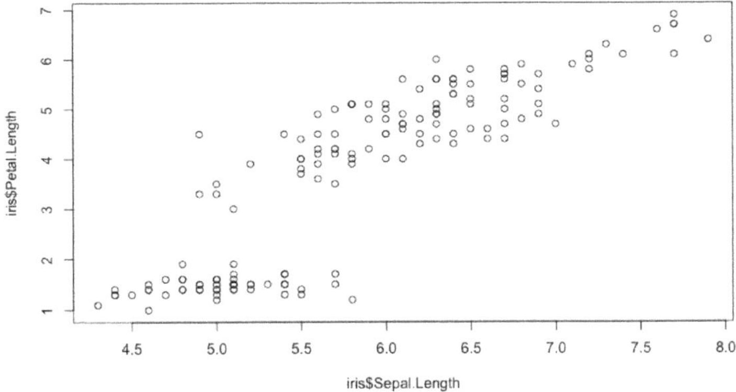

Chart 8.1.1 Scatter plot of the iris dataset [created by author].

The chart above is not very appealing. What is more, it has very limited options when it comes to adding layers. The most popular functions as an additional layer would be the lines() or points() functions.

```
lines(y, col="my_color")
```

8.2 GGPLOT2 framework and library

GGPLOT2 provides more customizable plotting features than the regular plot() function. This plotting method is based on multiple layers of information that is passed to the plotting engine. The layers can be envisioned as parts of a pyramid, with the most important element at the base.

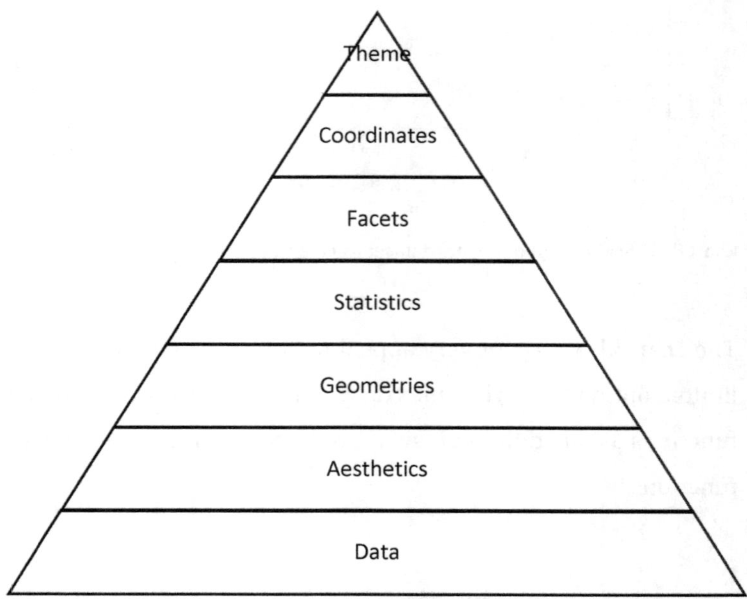

Picture 8.2.1 The GGPLOT2 framework pyramid [created by author].

The most important element of the ggplot framework, the **data**, points to the data frame that contains all the necessary data.

The **aesthetics** statement lists the X-axis and Y-axis variables and might specify the color variable if it doesn't depend on geometries.

Geometries specify the type of graphics for a given set of variables. Each geometry might have its own aesthetics. The most common geometries are:

- geom_bar – creates a bar chart,
- geom_point – creates a scatter plot,
- geom_jitter – creates a jitter plot,
- geom_abline – creates a line chart,
- geom_text – adds text for each coordinate specified in aesthetics,
- geom_rect – creates a plot with multiple rectangles,
- geom_polygon – creates a plot with polygons.

Multiple geometries can be combined on one graph. The "+" sign will combine the different layers:

```
ggplot(data=mydata, aes(x=x_var, y=y_var)) +
       geom_point(aes()) +
       geom_rug(aes())
```

When combining multiple geometries that have different statistics, the first ggplot() statement should be empty, allowing each consecutive geom_x statement to define new aesthetics:

```
gplot() +
  geom_point(data = df, aes(x = gp, y = y)) +
  geom_point(data = ds, aes(x = gp, y = mean),
          colour = 'red', size = 3) +
  geom_errorbar(data = ds, aes(x = gp, y = mean,
          ymin = mean - sd, ymax = mean + sd),
          colour = 'red', width = 0.4)
```

The three most important layers of this pyramid, described above can be found in any ggplot statement. The general ggplot template looks like this:

```
ggplot(df, aes(x = gp, y = y)) +
  geom_point() +
  geom_point(data = ds, aes(y = mean),
      colour = 'red', size = 3)
```

The coordinates statement in the ggplot framework defines the location of the geometries. We have a few coordinates statements that change the location of axes (source: http://sape.inf.usi.ch/quick-reference/ggplot2/coord, on 8/27/2018) :

- coord_cartesian - (default) cartesian coordinate system (x horizontal from left to right, y vertical from bottom to top),
- coord_flip - flipped cartesian coordinate system (x vertical from bottom to top, y horizontal from left to right),
- coord_polar - polar coordinate system; the x (or y) scale is mapped to the angle (theta),
- coord_map - various map projections.

```
ggplot(df, aes(x = gp, y = y)) +
  coord_flip()
```

The **theme** statement will provide the "feel and look" for the charts introducing grid lines, background color, etc. GGPLOT 2 has 2 built in themes:

- theme_grey() - the default theme, with a grey background,
- theme_bw() - white background.

The **facets** approach creates a matrix (grid) of plots. The main context in which the facets become useful is when there is another variable or two that we want to group the data by. There are two main **facets**:

- facet_wrap – when there is one variable based on which we want to create a strip of charts and wrap it,
- facet_grid – when there are two variables that we want to use to create the matrix.

Additional GGPLOT2 functions and tips can be found in the cheat sheet section in the appendix.

Let's consider the iris dataset that is available as a base dataset in R (no need to call any packages to load this data). In the below example, we want to create a scatter plot that shows the relationship between Sepal.Width and Sepal.Length. These two variables will be in our aesthetics layer. The geom_point() function will define the scatterplot type.

```
library(ggplot2)
ggplot(data=iris, aes(x=Sepal.Length, y=Sepal.Width))+
        geom_point()
```

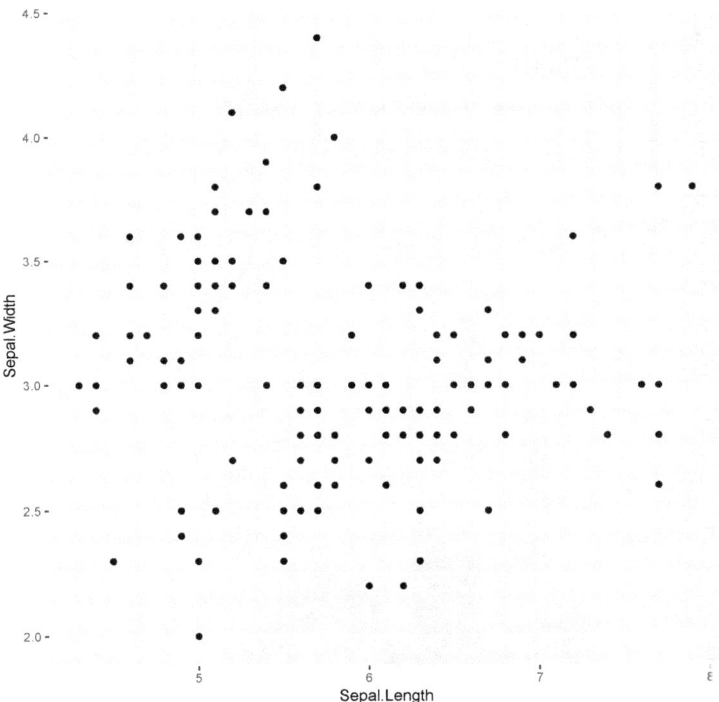

Picture 8.2.2 The GGPLOT2 scatterplot example with iris data [created by author].

The second example, showcased below, is a frequency histogram. Even though the chart looks like a bar chart, data scientists call it a frequency histogram because the height of the bar will indicate how many times a given value (on the X-axis) occurred in the particular variable. In this case, we use the geom_histogram() function to get a frequency histogram for the Sepal.Length variable.

```
library(ggplot2)
ggplot(data=iris, aes(Sepal.Length))+
  geom_histogram(binwidth=0.2)
```

The geom_histogram() function results in a chart show below.

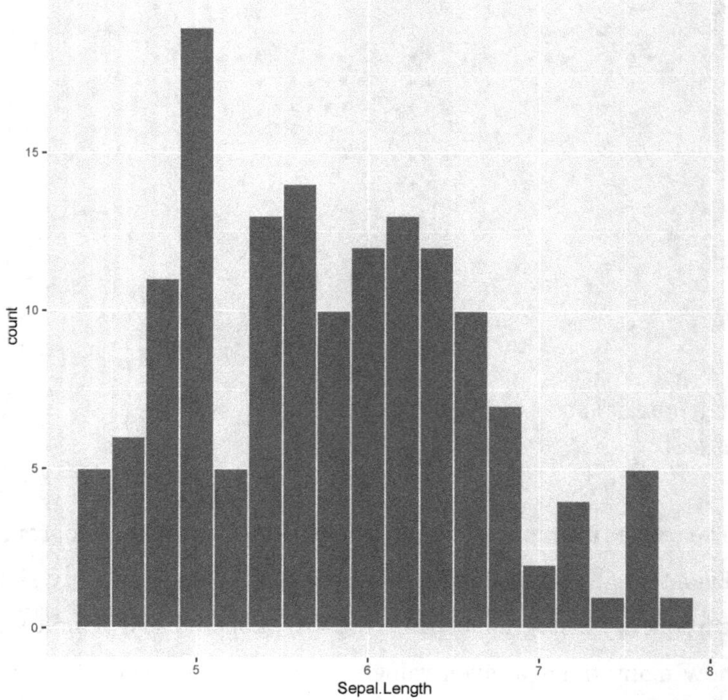

Picture 8.2.3 The GGPLOT2 scatterplot example with iris data [created by author].

8.3 Interactive visuals with Plotly

Plotly is a next generation engine for creating plots in R. The most important advantage of using Plotly is its interactivity. Zooming in and out, pane selection, lasso selection are only a few features available in Plotly. What is more, Plotly is a great framework for creating interactive dashboards in Shiny. (Shiny is a package that allows creating dashboards and web based applications.)

First, Plotly has many similarities to the ggplot. It has a main plotly() statement followed by specific geometries. All these statements are combined using "%>%" instead of using the "+" sign from ggplot.

```
install.packages("plotly")
library(plotly)
```

It is a good practice to create new objects with plotly charts and print them when finished. For a basic plotly box plot, the framework is as follows:

```
p <- plot_ly(data, x = ~x_var, color = ~y_var, type = "box")
p
```

Differently from the ggplot, plotly uses varaible names withe the approximation symbol "~".

In order to change the type of the plot, the "type" option needs to be changed. The most basic chart types are as follows:

- scatter plots,
- box plots,
- bar plots.

In order to combine multiple layers of geometries and add traces or points, to the base plot, the "%>%" needs to be applied:

```
p<-plot_ly(data, x= ~x_var, color= ~y_var, type = "box")
p <- p %>% add_trace( x=x, y = y2 )
p <- p %>% layout(legend =
                list( x = 0.5 ,
                y=1,
                bgcolor = '#F3F3F3' ))
p #this will print the p plot
```

Besides the "add_trace" function that is presented above, there are other functions that help adding geometries to the chart:

- add_lines – for adding lines to an existing chart,

```
%>% add_lines(y = ~fitted(loess(y_var ~ x_var)),
            line= list(color = 'rgba(7, 164, 181, 1)'),
```

```
                name ="my_name")
```

- add_markers – to add custom elements, aka. "markers",

```
%>% add_markers(y = ~y_var,
        text = optional,
        showlegend = FALSE)
```

- add_ribbons – to add a ribon to a line chart.

```
%>% add_ribbons(data = my_data,
        ymin = ~lower_band, ymax = ~upper_band,
        line = list(color = 'rgba(7, 164, 181, 0.05)'),
        fillcolor = 'rgba(7, 164, 181, 0.2)',
        name = "my_name")
```

When it comes to customizing chart elements, the best function is called marker(). This function needs to be included in the main plot_ly() function.

```
plot_ly(data = my_data, x = ~x_var, y = ~y_var,
        marker = list(size = 10,
                color = 'rgba(255, 182, 193, .9)',
                line = list(color = 'rgba(152, 0, 0, .8)',
                width = 2)))
```

When it comes to changing general chart display properties, the layout() function does all the work.

```
%>% layout(xaxis = list(title = 'x_name'),
        yaxis = list(title = 'y_title'),
      legend = list(x = 0.80, y = 0.90))
```

After running the plotly statements, the chart becomes available in the 4th, plot window. When the plot area is hovered over, a menu ribbon will pop-up in the upper right hand corner. A few icons will appear on the menu that do the following:

- zoom in and out,
- change the axes,
- provide a lasso selection,
- allow the user to add a tooltip when hovering over the chart elements and trace back the x and y values,
- return the original view.

In the example below, we are replicating the same chart that we created using ggplot in the previous chapter. It is a scatterplot that shows the relationship between the Sepal.Width and Sepal.Length.

```
library(plotly)
```

```
plot_ly(data=iris, x= iris$Sepal.Width,
        y= iris$Sepal.Length,
        color= iris$Sepal.Length,
        type = "scatter")
```

The above plotly code will produce a colorfull scatter plot with all the plotly functionalities as described in this chapter such as zoom in and out, lasso selection, changing access, etc. Those optionas are visible in the upper right hand corner after hovering over the chart with your mouse.

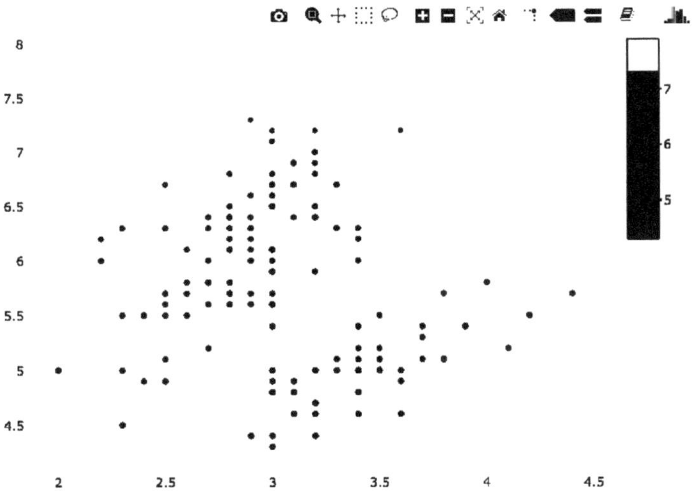

Picture 8.3.1 The Plotly scatterplot example with iris data [created by author].

8.4 Exercises

1. Using the plot() function, create one scatter plot for each pair of variables and frequency histograms (bar charts) for each variable separately:

a)Sepal.Length and Pedal.Width from the iris dataset,

b)Sepal.Width and Pedal.Length from the iris dataset,

c)Number and Age from the kyphosis dataset,

d) Age and Start from the kyphosis dataset,

e) Age and total.value from the dataset created in exercise 5.c from chapter 7,

f)Both variables in the cars dataset,

g**) The WFC stock and the SPY benchmark returns over the past 250 trading days (get the data using quantmod or quandl),

h**) The AAPL stock and the SPY benchmark returns over the past 250 trading days (get the data using quantmod or quandl).

2. Create ggplot plots for the following:

a) Scatter plot of Sepal.Width and Pedal.Width from the iris dataset,

b) Matrix of scatter plots for all the variables in the iris dataset using facets layer,

c) Scatter plot and a frequency histogram together on one plot for Age and Start from the kyphosis dataset,

d) Line chart for the price of AAPL stock from January 1st 2016 to September 1st 2018.

e**) Log returns for any equity mutual fund for the period from January 1st 2015 to December 31st 2017.

3.Decide what chart type is best and create ggplots for the following data elements for the titanic_train dataset from the library(titanic):

a) Fare against age,

b) Median age per pclass,

c) Sum of fair per pclass and sex,

d) Survived status against sex.

4.Recode the plots from exercise 2 in plot_ly. Analyze the plots using plot_ly's features.

5.Recode the plots from exercise 3 in plot_ly.

a) Zoom in on any outliers and try to understand why these are outliers. Make screen shots of the zoomed in charts.

6.A hardware store chain has 30 stores. Each store generates daily revenue that is normally distributed over time (rnorm() function). Using a *for loop* to run a simulation of each store, plot the timeseries using the plotly framework.

7.You are the data and analytics manager of a Fortune 500 company. Last week, you surveyed all the customer facing employees in the company's headquarters and noticed that their total compensation is based on two factors: years with the company and generated revenue. Fit a second degree polynomial function to predict the salary on the data.

salary	years_w_company	generated_rev
216,344.77	8	85,013.09
242,226.87	5	95,593.11
29,487.10	8	8,742.88
216,246.57	4	84,991.58
20,905.48	4	5,261.64
181,123.01	5.5	70,650.01
129,937.99	8	49,742.34
293,054.30	10	116,310.37
39,758.87	1.5	12,961.83
111,967.53	4.5	42,427.36
10,990.51	4.5	1,212.31
33,739.11	5.5	10,492.97
200,791.05	4	78,684.40
273,329.40	0.5	108,297.71
111,807.44	10	42,329.69
109,325.17	8	41,333.31
258,285.53	4	102,151.64
81,401.51	1	29,959.25
258,794.62	4	102,358.47

Plot the relationships between the variables side by side, using the plotly framework.

8.Using ggplot(), create frequency histograms (bar charts) for each variable from the Horse Colic Data Set that can be found at https://archive.ics.uci.edu/ml/datasets.html

9.Using plotly(), create timeseries plots to explain the evolvement of El Nino patterns over time. Consider humidity, temperature, subsurface temperatures. Are there any correlations that need to be explained (use scatter plots to understand correlations)? Use the El Nino Data Set from the https://archive.ics.uci.edu/ml/datasets.html website.

9. Building a dashboard in R Shiny

9.1 Shiny as a framework

Shiny is a great tool to build an interactive dashboard or web-based user interface for almost any visuals, tables, or text outputs. Shiny also allows the user to modify the data inputs and parameters.

The basic Shiny framework is based on two files:

- server file, that has all the data manipulation, and analysis logic,
- ui file, that stores the entire design of the user interface.

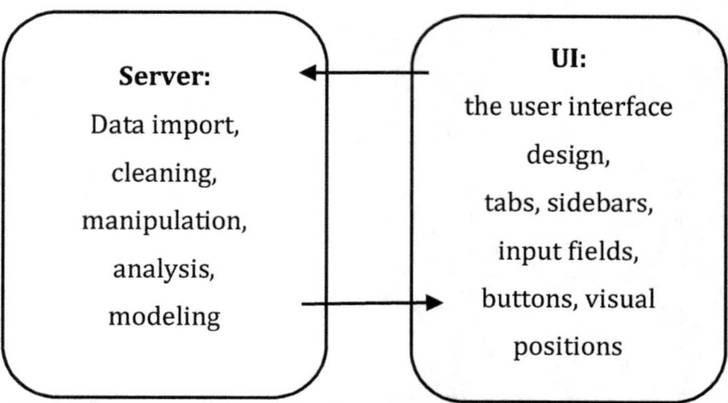

Picture 9.1.1 The general R Shiny framework [created by author].

To open a Shiny framework, click on the "new script" icon with the green plus sign in the upper left-hand side corner and click on the Shiny Web App option. This will open a pop-up window will a few options. The first one will ask the user to provide an application name. The application name is not very important at this point and we can provide any random name. The second selection is Single File or Multiple File. It is recommended to work in the "Multiple File" mode. The third option needs the user to specify the directory where the files will be saved. Both files, the Server.R and UI.R need to be saved in the same directory.

Two new scripts will open in the "script window" after clicking OK in the Shiny pop up window. The two new files are called:

- Server.R,
- UI.R.

These two files will have default templates that can be easily modified for any custom project.

9.2 Server and UI interaction

Even though the Server.R and UI.R are separate files, they are required to have common elements.

The server can do all the work related to importing and manipulating/transforming the data. However, in the end it has to create objects that are readable by the UI.R file. These objects can be created using the following functions:

- renderImage() – creates a static image for the UI,
- renderPlot() – takes simple plots and ggplots,
- renderPrint() – builds and object with text or console outputs,
- renderTable() – stores a data frame,
- renderText() – stores static text,
- renderPlotly() – stores plotly charts.

These functions work just like the user defined functions and need to return an object that has the specific type.

What is more, each of these objects has to be named using the following template:

```
output$name <- renderTable()
```

Each server function listed above has a matching function for the UI.R file:

- renderImage() – imageOutput(),
- renderPlot() – plotOutput(),
- renderPrint() – verbatimTextOutput(),
- renderTable() – tableOutput(),

- renderText() – textOutput(),
- renderPlotly() – plotlyOutput().

The UI.R file will use the *name* defined in the Server.R as function input for the corresponding UI function.

9.3 Basic server functions

There are many server side functions that give outputs for the UI. It would be impossible to list out all of the functions in this chapter. However, we'll take a look at the renderPlot() function to understand how Shiny creates objects. Please remember that each render function needs to be saved as an **OUTPUT** object using the following template:

> **output**$*obj_name* <- renderPlot()

The renderPlot() function has a very detailed description with many options that can be found on the shiny website [source: www.shiny.rstudio.com]. Despite all the available options, using the function below is more than enough.

> output$myplot <- renderPlot(*expr*, width = "*auto*", > height = "*auto*")

Where:

width – is the width of the plot, can be "auto" or a fixed dimension,

height – is the height of the plot, and can be fixed as well,

expr- are all the regular R expressions that create the plot, this could be a plot(x) function or a set of functions that lead to creating a ggplot object. In the case of using a ggplot framework, the object needs to be saved in the global environment (e.g. P) and then called at the end of the code, like this:

```
output$myplot <- renderPlot(
        P <- ggplot(data=xyz, aes(x=x, y=y)+
                geom_lines(...)
        print(P)
, width = "auto", height = "auto")# closing renderPlot
```

9.4 UI elements and user inputs

The UI.R will have two types of objects/functions:

- user inputs – multiple choice boxes, date inputs, text inputs, radioButtons, actionButtons, etc,
- server output – any function like plotOutput(), textOutput(), etc., that referes to an object created in the server.

The "server output" functions have been listed at the end of chapter 9.2. These xyzOutput() functions require an object name that was created in the server using a corresponding "server side" function.

On the other hand, the user inputs will create objects that the server can easily read using a template:

> input$*ui_input_name*

The most basic user inputs include:
- actionButton(),
- checkboxGroupInput(),
- checkboxInput(),
- dateInput(),
- fileInput(),
- radioButtons(),
- textInput(),
- sliderInput().

More functions for the UI.R and Server.R can be found in the Appendix in the R Shiny Cheat Sheet.

One of the most important features that R Shiny has is the ability to modify the layout of the UI. In order to manage the end user experience, Shiny allows to create tabs, menus, sidebars, etc. , just like in HTML.

There are 5 basic ways to organize panels:

- sidebarLayout – the most popular

```
ui <- fluidPage(
 sidebarLayout(
        sidebarPanel(),
        mainPanel()
 )#closing sidebarLayout
 )#closing fluidPage
```

- splitLayout

```
ui <- fluidPage(
 splitLayout(
        object1, object2,.....
 )#closing splitLayout
 )#closing fluidPage
```

- verticalLayout

```
ui <- fluidPage(
 verticalLayout(
        object1, object2,.....
 )#closing verticalLayout
 )#closing fluidPage
```

- flowLayout

```
ui <- fluidPage(
flowLayout(
        object1, object2,......
)#closing flowLayout
)#closing fluidPage
```

- fluidRow

```
ui <- fluidPage(
fluidRow(column(), column()),
fluidRow(column(),column())
)#closing fluidPage
```

What is more, each Layout can contain multiple tabs. The tabsetPanel function controls the dynamics of tabs.

```
ui <- fluidPage(tabsetPanel(
tabPanel("tab1", content),
tabPanel("tab2", content)
)#closing tabsetPanel
)#closing fluidPage
```

Finally, the graph below visualizes how the objects and information flow from the UI to server and back to the UI.

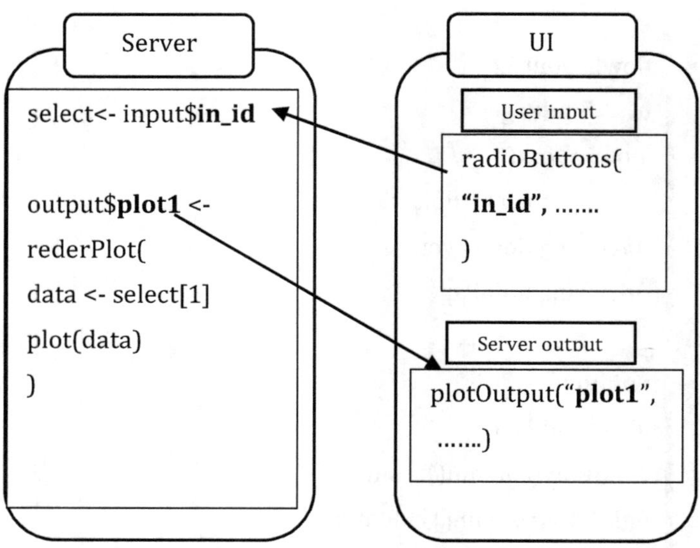

Picture 9.4.1 Information flow between UI and SERVER [created by author].

9.5 Exercises – R Shiny project

Project 1. Create a web-based application that uses the kyphosis dataset and allows the user to select two variables (create two drop down selection boxes). The application creates a ggplot scatterplot for any given set of two variables.

Project 2. Using the titanic_train dataset from the library(titanic), create a web based application with a sidebar and two tabs. The sidebar has:

a) a sliderInput() that allows to subset the age variable.

b) radiobuttons that subset the sex variable

The first tab will have a plotly() graph of Age and Fare for all remaining observations, based on the selections from the sidebar. Tab two will have a logistic regression summary() for a model that predicts if the person survived.

Project 3**. Recode project 2 using library(shinydashboard) approach. Make sure to use two or three valueBox() objects on the landing page and provide some basic statistics for the titanic dataset. Use appropriate icons in all valueBox() objects.

10. Report automation in R Markdown

10.1 R Markdown setup and basic features

R Markdown is a great tool for report automation. It can generate reports in a few formats:

- HTML - same styling capabilities as regular HTML websites and CSS styling can be applied as well,
- PDF – less styling options, easier to distribute via email,
- other – including a MS Word document (these need additional packages and will not be covered in this chapter).

A new Markdown project can be opened by clicking the "new script" icon with the green plus sign in the upper left corner. When the drop down list comes up, select the "R Markdown..." option. A pop-up window will appear with a few fields to fill out. In this chapter we'll use the "Document" option from the left-hand side list.

10.1 R Markdown setup and basic features

New R Markdown

Document

Presentation

Shiny

From Template

Title: Untitled

Author:

Default Output Format:

HTML

Recommended format for authoring (you can switch to PDF or Word output anytime).

PDF

PDF output requires TeX (MiKTeX on Windows, MacTeX 2013+ on OS X, TeX Live 2013+ on Linux).

Word

Previewing Word documents requires an installation of MS Word (or Libre/Open Office on Linux).

OK | Cancel |

Picture 10.1.1 R Markdown Wizard [created by author].

We highly recommend that you explore the other options that are listed, such as "Presentation" or "From Template". In the other fields, you will need to provide the document name or title, author, and the document type using the radio buttons. Select the HTML document type for your first R Markdown project.

10.2 Code chunks and types in Markdown

When all the steps from chapter 10.1 are completed, a script template with the following code chunks will open:

```
---
title: "Untitled"
output: html_document
---

```{r setup, include=FALSE}
knitr::opts_chunk$set(echo = TRUE)
```

R Markdown

This is an R Markdown document. Markdown is a simple formatting syntax for authoring HTML, PDF, and MS Word documents. For more details on using R Markdown see <http://rmarkdown.rstudio.com>.

When you click the **Knit** button a document will be generated that includes both content as well as the output of any embedded R code chunks within the document. You can embed an R code chunk like this:
```

```
```{r cars}
summary(cars)
```
```

The first few lines, separated from the other code using ---
(dashes), with the title and output statements are called the
header. The header contains basic information about the
Markdown document such as the title, author name, date, and
type (HTML, PDF, or other). It might also have a reference line to
a .css file with all the formatting styles for a HTML document.

The second chunk is where the R code is stored. This chunk will
execute just like any regular R code and output only the object
that is printed. The printed output can be a plot, model summary,
data frame, etc. This chunk has to be surrounded by ``` and the {r
options} indicates if the errors and warnings need to be printed.

```
```{r setup, include=FALSE}
knitr::opts_chunk$set(echo = TRUE)
```
```

In the initial Markdown script, the following statement is included:

> ## R Markdown

Markdown understands #, ##, ### as styling references and will print the following text as a header in the final output document.

Finally, Markdown can print simple text to the final output document. It doesn't need any special characters around it and will print the text using default font.

Once your Markdown script is ready and has all the code chunks, click the drop down next to the "Knit" icon and select the appropriate document type. This will produce the final output document.

10.3 Exercises – R Shiny project **

Project 1. Using the scatterplots from Project 1 in chapter 9. Create a report with scatterplots for all pairs of variables and provide short descriptions for each scatter plot.

Project 2. Use the plot and model summary from Project 2 in chapter 9. Create a report that will describe the plot and the model summary. Focus your descriptions on the significance of variables.

11. List of most useful functions

11.1 Mathematical

log(x),logb(),log10(),log2(),exp(),expm1(),log1p(),sqrt()

cos(),sin(),tan(),acos(),asin(),atan(),atan2()

cosh(),sinh(),tanh(),acosh(),asinh(),atanh()

union(),intersect(),setdiff(),setequal()

Basic operators:

+,-,*,/,^,%%,%/%

Comparison operators:

<,>,<=,>=,==,!=

Principal component analysis, eigenvectors and eigenvalues:

eigen() , princomp()

Calculus:

deriv()

integrate()

sqrt(),sum()

11.2 Data manipulation

read_csv()

read_tsv()

read_delim()

read_fwf()

read_table()

as.data.frame()

as.numeric()

as.character()

as.Date()

na.omit()   -excludes all the rows with at least one missing

is.na()   -tests an object for being empty

t()   -transposes a matrix

gsub()   -replaces a given string with a new string

subset()   -subsets a data frame based on a value

which()   -gives indexes based on a condition

extract()   -Extract one column into multiple columns.

gather()   -Gather columns into key-value pairs.

nest()   -nest a few columns together

separate()   -Separate one column into multiple columns.

separate_rows()-Separate a collapsed column into multiple rows.

unite()   -Unite multiple columns into one.

drop_na()   -Drop rows containing missing values

fill()   -Fill in missing values.

replace_na()   -Replace missing values

11.3 Regression, optimization, and fitting

lm()	-linear modeling
glm()	-generalizes linear modeling
nls()	-non linear leased squares
predict()	-gives prediction for most models
summary()	-provides a summary for a model
optim()	-general optimization
optimize()	-1 dimentional optimization
nlm()	-non linear minimization
nlmLM()	-non linear minimization, more options

11.4 Descriptive statistics

mean()
sum()
median()
sd()
colMeans()
percentile()
summary()

12. Data mining with MongoDB (noSQL)

In one of the previous chapters, we've explained how to use SQL to combine, analyze, and subset data. Those SQL queries work very well on relational data that is linked by primary and secondary keys. However, more and more data is stored in non-relational databases, that use the NoSQL language. Non-relational databases can be created to host different objects such as documents, keys, graphs, pictures, etc. and do not require defining relationships between the data objects.

12.1 Installing MongoDB

MongoDB is a database that combines both concepts, the capabilities of relational databases, and the flexibility of NoSQL. What is more, Mongo DB is a free, open source database that runs on a NoSQL engine. The data behind it is saved in a JSON format. The first step to start using MongoDB is to install the software. The drivers can be installed on a macOS, Windows, or Linux and come in two editions:

- Community Edition – is a free open source version,
- Enterprise – provides more security and encryption but has a cost associated with it.

There are different steps for installing MongoDB on different operating systems. A full list of instructions for each operating system can be found at https://docs.mongodb.com/manual/installation/

For the macOS, the instructions are as follows [source: https://docs.mongodb.com/manual/tutorial/install-mongodb-on-os-x/ , on 8/24/2018] :

Install MongoDB Community Edition Manuall:

Step 1:

Download the MongoDB .tar.gz tarball.

- Download the tarball for your system from the MongoDB Download Center https://www.mongodb.com/download-center#production

Step 2:

Extract the files from the downloaded archive.

- Submit the following statement in your terminal:

    tar -zxvf mongodb-osx-ssl-x86_64-4.0.1.tgz

Step 3:

Ensure the binaries are in a directory listed in your PATH environment variable. The MongoDB binaries are in the **bin/** directory of the tarball. You must either:

- Copy these binaries into a directory listed in your PATH variable such as **/usr/local/bin**,
- Create symbolic links to each of these binaries from a directory listed in your PATH variable, or
- Modify your user's PATH environment variable to include this directory.

For example, you can add the following line to your shell's initialization script (e.g. **~/.bashrc**):

> Export PATH=<mongodb-install-directory>/bin:$PATH

Replace **<mongodb-install-directory>** with the path to the extracted MongoDB archive.

12.2 Installing MongoDB Community with Homebrew

The instructions below are copied from the official MongoDB website: https://docs.mongodb.com/manual/tutorial/install-mongodb-on-os-x/

12.2 Installing MongoDB Community with Homebrew

Homebrew installs binary packages based on published "formulae." This section describes how to update brew to the latest packages and install MongoDB Community Edition. Homebrew requires some initial setup and configuration, which is beyond the scope of this document.

Step 1:

Update Homebrew's package database.

In a system shell, issue the following command:

```
brew update
```

Step 2:

Install MongoDB.

You can install MongoDB via brew with several different options. Use one of the following operations:

- Install the MongoDB Binaries

  To install the MongoDB binaries, issue the following command in a system shell:

  ```
  brew install mongodb
  ```

- Install the Latest Development Release of MongoD3

To install the latest development release for use in testing and development, issue the following command in a system shell:

```
brew install mongodb --devel
```

12.3 Running MongoDB

The following steps will boot Mongo DB:

Step 1:

Create the data directory.

Before you start MongoDB for the first time, create the directory to which the mongod process will write data. By default, the mongod process uses the /data/db directory. If you create a directory other than this one, you must specify that directory in the dbpath option when starting the mongod process later in this procedure.

The following example command creates the default **/data/db directory:**

```
mkdir -p /data/db
```

Step 2:

Set permissions for the data directory.

Before running mongod for the first time, ensure that the user account running mongod has read and write permissions for the directory.

Step 3:

Run MongoDB.

To run MongoDB, run the **mongod** process at the system prompt. If necessary, specify the path of the **mongod** or the data directory. See the following examples:

- Run without specifying paths

  If your system PATH variable includes the location of the mongod binary and if you use the default data directory (i.e., /data/db), simply enter mongod at the system prompt:

  ```
  mongod
  ```

- Specify the path of the mongod

  If your PATH does not include the location of the mongod binary, enter the full path to the mongod binary at the system prompt:

  ```
  <path to binary>/mongod
  ```

- Specify the path of the data directory

  If you do not use the default data directory (i.e., /data/db), specify the path to the data directory using the --dbpath option:

```
mongod --dbpath <path to data directory>
```

Step 4:

Verify that MongoDB has started successfully.

Verify that MongoDB has started successfully by checking the process output for the following line:

```
[initandlisten] waiting for connections on port 27017
```

The output should be visible in the terminal or shell window.

You may see non-critical warnings in the process output. As long as you see the log line shown above, you can safely ignore these warnings during your initial evaluation of MongoDB.

Step 5:

Begin using MongoDB.

Start a mongo shell on the same host machine as the mongod. Use the **--host** command line option to specify the localhost address (in this case 127.0.0.1) and port that the mongod listens on:

```
mongo --host 127.0.0.1:27017
```

Later, to stop MongoDB, press Control+C in the terminal where the mongod instance is running.

12.4 Using MongoDB from R

The best package for establishing a connection with MongoDB from R is the mongolite library.

```
install.packages("mongolite")
library(mongolite)
```

If the MongoDB that you're trying to access is on your computer, you must start it by running the following in your shell:

```
mogod
```

Once we have our database up and running we will have to create our first connection, database, and collection. The mongo() function will create a collection:

```
my_collection = mongo(collection =
                    "collection_name",
```

```
                                        db = "db_name")
```

12.5 Uploading files to MongoDB

The easiest way to upload data to a collection defined in chapter 12.4 is to use the $insert options.

```
my_collection$insert(my_data)
```

12.6 Managing non-relational data using NoSQL

MongoDB uses JSON based syntax to manage the data. There are a few basic functions, including the **$find** function, that take JSON syntax as arguments.

```
my_new_data <- my_collection$find(
query = '{"field1" : "field1_val", "field3" : { "$lt" : 100 } }',
fields = '{"field1" : true, "field2" : true}',
limit = 5
)
```

The above query filters **($find)** *field1* based on the *field1_val*. The "query" statement has all the filters, whereas the "fields" section lists all variables that are supposed to be printed. The "limit" puts a limit on the number of rows that get carried over to the new table.

When it comes to aggregating data **($aggregate)**, the JSON syntax requires one of the following aggregation names such as **$sum, $avg, $count**, etc. and the **$group** reference.

```
my_new_data <- my_collection$aggregate(
 '[{"$group":{"_id":"$carrier","count":{"$sum":1},
"average":{"$avg":"$distance"}}}]',
 options = '{"allowDiskUse":true}'
)
```

MongoDB allows to use a more flexible aggregation method called "mapreduce". Mapreduce uses JavaScript language to call more complex aggregations in MongoDB. Unless you know JavaScript, it is recommended to pull raw data from MongoDB to R and perform operations in R using R functions.

12.7 Exercises

1. Move the following datasets to the MongoDB and create new collections:

a) iris,

b) kyphosis.

2 Get the following from the kyphosis collection from MongoDB:

a) All the variables and all the observations,

b) Just the Number and Age variables and all the observations,

c) All the variables and only the observations that have Age greater than 50,

d) Just the Number and Age variables and only the observations that have Age smaller than 40,

e) Just the Kyphosis variable for all the observations with Number smaller than 5.

3. Get the following from the iris collection from MongoDB:

a) All the variables and all the observations,

b) Just the Sepal.Length and Sepal.Width variables and all the observations ,

c) All the variables and only the observations that have Sepal.Length greater than 4,

d) Just the Pedal.Length and Sepal.Width variables and only the observations that have Sepal.Length smaller than 4,

e) Just the Sepal.Length variable for all the observations with Sepal.Width smaller than 4.

4. Get the following from the kyphosis collection from MongoDB:

a) All the observations. Aggregate the data to get the sum of Age per each kyphosis outcome,

b) All the observations. Aggregate the data to get the arithmetic mean of Age per each kyphosis outcome,

c) Observations that have Age greater than 50. Aggregate the data to get the count of observations per each kyphosis outcome,

d) Observations that have Age smaller than 40. Aggregate the data to get the count of distinct Number values per each kyphosis outcome,

e) Observations with Number smaller than 5. Aggregate the data to get the count of distinct Number values per each kyphosis outcome.

5**. Get the following from the iris collection from MongoDB:

a) All the observations. Aggregate the data to get the sum of Petal.Length per each Species group,

b) All the observations. Aggregate the data to get the arithmetic mean of Petal.Width per each Species group,

c) Observations that have Petal.Length greater than 3.5. Aggregate the data to get the count of observations per each Species group,

d) Observations that have Sepal.Width smaller than 3.4. Aggregate the data to get the count of distinct Sepal.Length values per each Species group,

e) Observations with Petal.Length smaller than 1.8. Aggregate the data to get the count of distinct Petal.Width values per each Species group.

13. Text analytics

13.1 Importing data and creating a text corpus

Text analytics requires uploading multiple data files, such as .pdf or .doc files. Each file is treated as a separate observation.

To upload multiple .pdf files we will use the library(tm):

```
install.packages("tm")
library(tm)
```

Move all the .pdf files to one location that is somewhere locally, on your computer and run the following function to get all the .pdf file names in the specified directory.

```
files <- list.files(path="my_path",pattern = "pdf$")
```

Once you have created a list with all the document names, you'll need to import all the documents into the R environment. To import the .pdf files, we'll need to create an "engine" function that can be used when creating a text corpus.

```
install.packages("pdftools")
library(pdftools)
```

13.1 Importing data and creating a text corpus

```
Rpdf <- readPDF(control = list(text = "-layout"))
```

The readPDF() function listed above creates a user defined function, the "engine", and saves it in the environment. This function does not import the data.

Next, we'll use the "engine" function to import the Corpus (a Corpus is an object will all the data from all the documents):

```
my_corpus <- Corpus(URISource(files),
        readerControl = list(reader = Rpdf))
```

The process for importing text files is slightly different from the .pdf importing process explained above. Text files are much easier to read as they store information about each character and string that is included in the file.

The main difference between importing .pdf and .doc file is the reader options. For .pdf files, we have to create a readPDF() function, whereas the readDOC reader is used for .doc files.

```
files1 <- list.files(path="my_path",pattern = ".doc")
ex_eng <- Corpus(URISource(files1),
        readerControl=list(reader=readDOC,
                language='en_CA',
                load=TRUE))
```

13.2 Term-document matrix (TDM)

In chapter 13.1, we've explained how to create a Corpus using multiple .pdf and .doc files. With such a data structure we should be able to convert all the documents from the Corpus into a **term-document matrix (TDM)**. The TDM is a large matrix with all the tokens (term "token" stands for one "word") found in all documents with frequencies. We can use the following function from the library(tm):

```
my_tdm <- TermDocumentMatrix(my_corpus,
control = list(removePunctuation = TRUE,
                          stopwords = TRUE,
                          tolower = TRUE,
                          stemming = TRUE,
                          removeNumbers = TRUE))
```

The TermDocumentMatrix() has many options that allow to clean up the Corpus. It is highly recommended to build the TDM with options that exclude all punctuation, upper/lower case variations of the same word, and numbers.

Alternatively, the TDM can be cleaned up using the tm_map() function:

```
my_tdm <- tm_map(my_tdm, stripWhitespace)
my_tdm <- tm_map(my_tdm,
content_transformer(tolower))
my_tdm <- tm_map(my_tdm, removeWords,
stopwords("english"))
```

The tm_map() with removeWords, stopwords() option will remove all the words that do not make sense to analyze, such as: I, we, he, she, is, are, being, etc.

The inspect() function will analyze the TDM. What is more, this function can be subset the TDM just like any other matrix using indexes for rows and columns, or column names (column names or row names will have the tokens). The outcome will print a frequency table (how many times a word was used) for all the tokens.

```
inspect(my_tdm)
```

Other useful functions used to analyze the TDM are:

```
findFreqTerms(my_tdm, frequency_count)
findAssocs(my_tdm, "my_word", correlation)
```

The first function will print all the words for a given frequency. The *frequency_count* has to be an integer greater than 0.

The second function will print all the words that are associated with *my_word* at a given *correlation* (number between 0 and 1).

13.3 Get sentiments from tidytext

The very well-known package called tidytext offers sentimental token classification. It will assign a negative or positive label to all the tokens that are available in the library.

First, the TDM had to be transformed using the tidy() function:

```
library(dplyr)
library(tidytext)


tidy_tdm <- tidy(my_tdm)
```

Next, we need to left join the sentiment data from library(tidytext) using the get_sentiments() function. The following code joins the two:

```
tdm_sentiments <- tidy_tdm %>%
  inner_join(get_sentiments("bing"), by = c(term = "word"))
```

After joining the sentiments to the TDM data, we can run basic analytics to find the most negative documents in our TDM[source: https://cran.r-project.org/web/packages/tidytext/vignettes/tidying_casting.html on 8/10/2018]:

```
library(tidyr)

tdm_sentiments %>%
  count(document, sentiment, wt = count) %>%
  spread(sentiment, n, fill = 0) %>%
  mutate(sentiment = positive - negative) %>%
  arrange(sentiment)
```

We can also create a visual that gives frequencies of the most positive and most negative tokens in our TDM [source: https://cran.r-project.org/web/packages/tidytext/vignettes/tidying_casting.html on 8/10/2018]:

```
library(ggplot2)

tdm_sentiments %>%
  count(sentiment, term, wt = count) %>%
```

```
filter(n >= 150) %>%
mutate(n = ifelse(sentiment == "negative", -n, n)) %>%
mutate(term = reorder(term, n)) %>%

ggplot(aes(term, n, fill = sentiment)) +
geom_bar(stat = "identity") +
theme(axis.text.x = element_text(angle = 90, hjust = 1))
```

The ggplot statement will give the following bar chart:

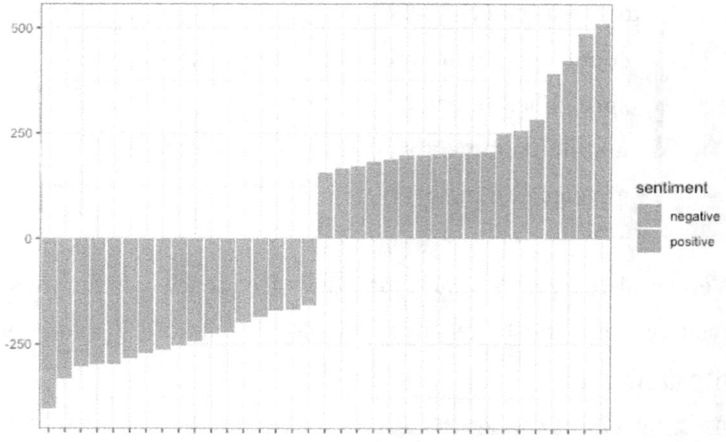

Picture 13.3.1 Negative and positive token frequency [created by author].

13.4 Creating word clouds

Word clouds are probably the worst type of plots used to visualize text frequencies. Nevertheless they are used very often and need to be described in this chapter.

Since word clouds are so popular, a package called wordcloud was created. The package has a function called wordcloud() that creates the word cloud based on the tokens and the frequencies. Before we introduce the wordcloud() function, we need to manipulate the TDM so that it becomes a sorted data frame. Here are the following steps:

- Convert the TDM to a matrix,
- Sort the matrix by decreasing frequency of the tokens,
- Create a data frame with tokens and frequencies.

The following template can be used to manipulate the TDM object (we'll use the my_tdm object created in chapter 13.3):

```
p <- as.matrix(my_tdm)
v <- sort(rowSums(p),decreasing=TRUE)
final_df <- data.frame(word = names(v),freq=v)
```

The final step is to use the transformed data frame called final_df in the wordcloud() function.

```
wordcloud(words = final_df $word,
        freq = final_df $freq, min.freq = 1,
      max.words=200, random.order=FALSE,
    rot.per=0.35,  colors=brewer.pal(8, "Dark2"))
```

13.5 Bayesian text classification model

Some documents might be classified into groups. In most cases the groups can be labeled as 1 for all the "yes", "present", etc. groups and 0 for the "no", "absent" groups. In this case we can build a supervised learning model based on Bayesian inference.

First, we need to make sure that our TDM is a matrix and that we have a "y" (label) variable for each document in this matrix.

```
tdm_matrix <- as.matrix(my_tdm)
tdm_matrix1 <- cbind(tdm_matrix, c(0,1))
colnames(tdm_matrix1)[ncol(tdm_matrix1)] <- y
tdm_matrix1 <- as.data.frame(tdm_matrix1)
tdm_matrix1$y <- as.factor(tdm_matrix1$y)
```

The tdm_matrix1 is a data frame with binary labels, called the "y" variable. The "y" variable needs to be a factor to work in the next step. In the next step, we will fit a Bayesian model on the data to get a predictive framework.

```
Library(caret)
baysian1 <- train(y ~ ., data = tdm_matrix1,
        method = 'bayesglm')
```

Once we fit the model, we can use the predict() function to predict the "y" label for any new documents.

13.6 Exercise

1. Using the AssociatedPress documents from library(topicmodels), analyze the TDM and look for most frequent tokens. Hint: after installing the topicmodels package, run the following code:

```
data("AssociatedPress", package = "topicmodels")
```

2. Using the TDM created in exercise 1, find the sentiments using library(tidytext).

a) Plot a word cloud for all the tokens that have a positive sentiment,

b) Plot a word cloud for all the tokens that have a negative sentiment.

3.Create a Bayesian text classification model based on the documents used in exercise 2.

a)What are the model parameters,

b)What can you tell about the model significance.

14. Appendix

14.1 READR cheat sheet [source: rstudio.com]

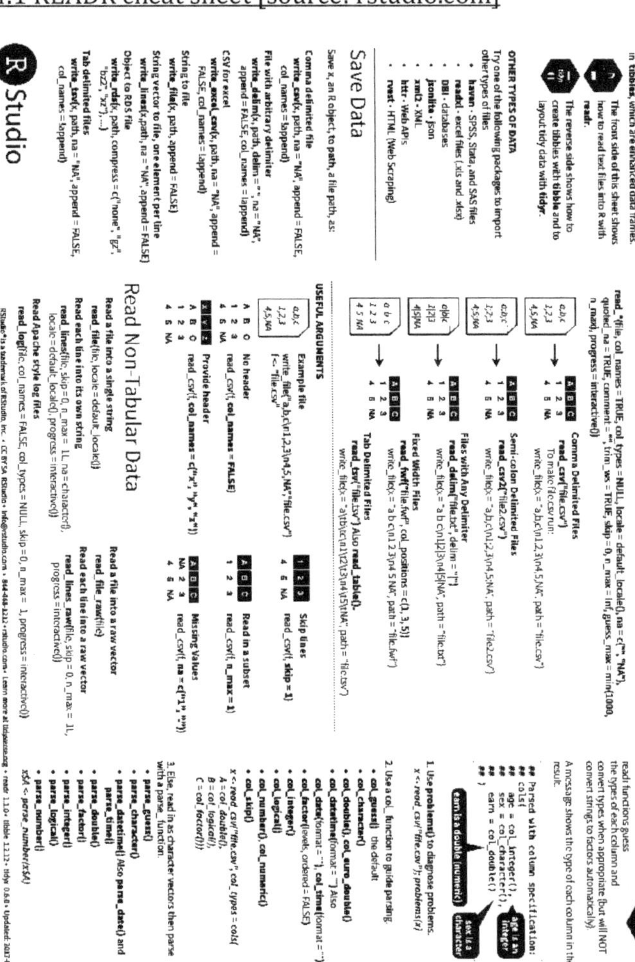

14.2 GGPLOT2 cheat sheet [source: rstudio.com]

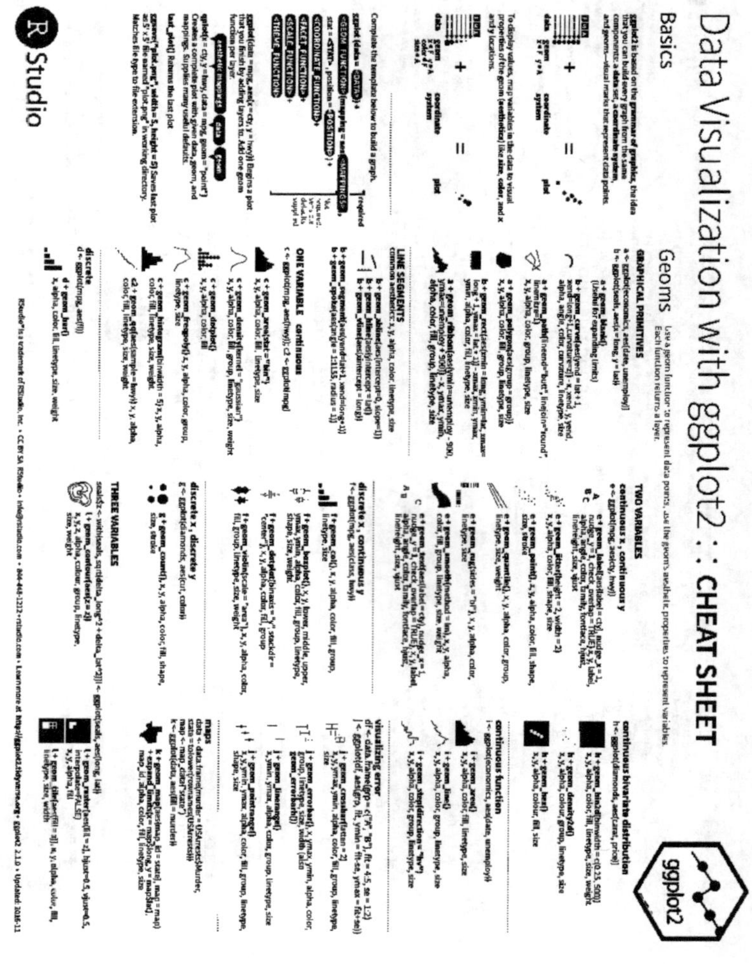

14.3 R SHINY cheat sheet [source: rstudio.com]

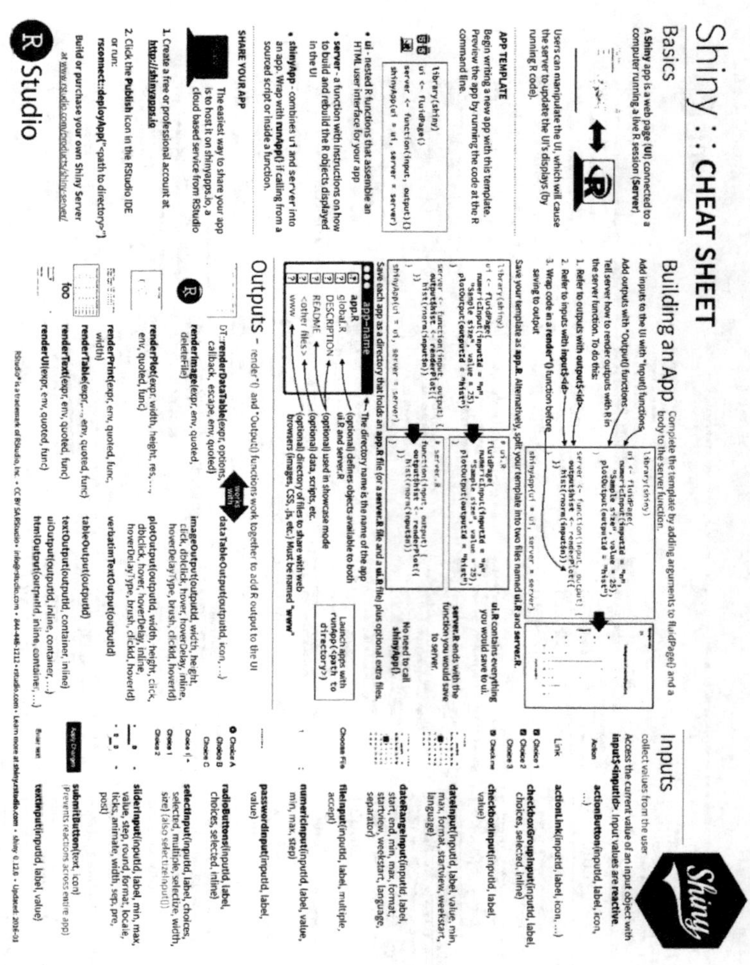

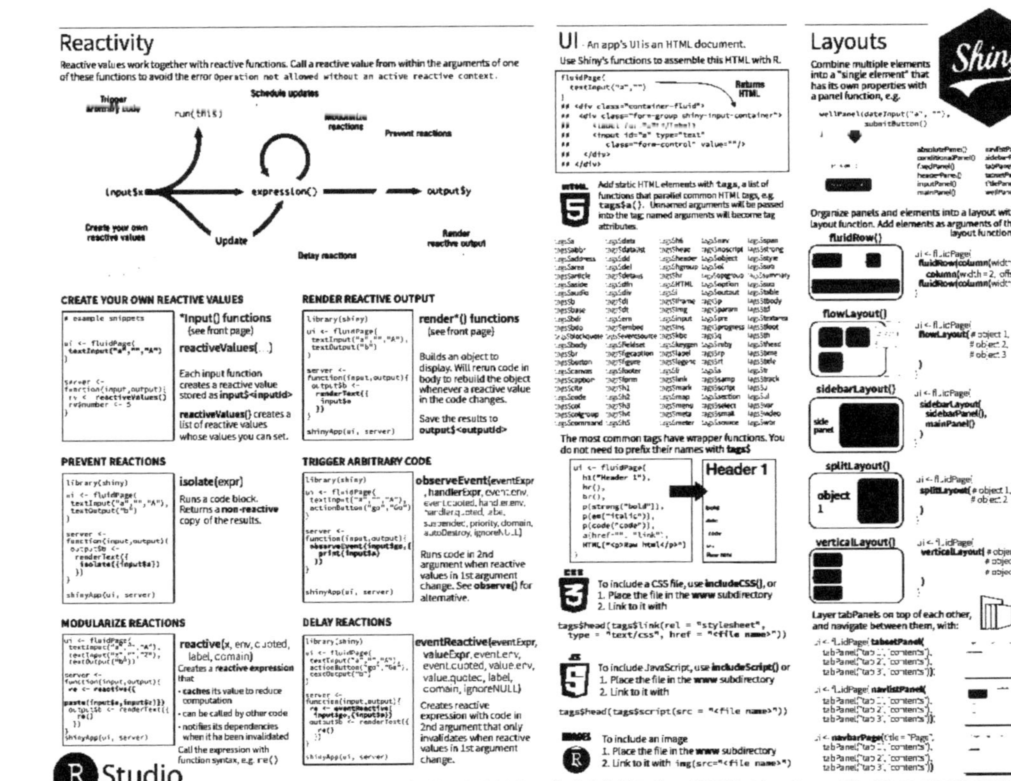

Reactivity
Reactive values work together with reactive functions. Call a reactive value from within the arguments of one of these functions to avoid the error Operation not allowed without an active reactive context.

Trigger arbitrary code
run(this)
Schedule updates
modularize reactions
Prevent reactions
input$x
expression()
output$y
Create your own reactive values
Update
Delay reactions
Render reactive output

CREATE YOUR OWN REACTIVE VALUES
# example snippets
ui <- fluidPage(
  textInput("a","","A")
)
server <-
function(input,output){
  rv < reactiveValues()
  rv$number <- 5
}

*Input() functions
(see front page)
reactiveValues(...)
Each input function creates a reactive value stored as input$<inputId>
reactiveValues() creates a list of reactive values whose values you can set.

RENDER REACTIVE OUTPUT
library(shiny)
ui <- fluidPage(
  textInput("a","","A"),
  textOutput("b")
)
server <-
function(input,output){
  output$b <-
    renderText({
      input$a
    })
}
shinyApp(ui, server)

render*() functions
(see front page)
Builds an object to display. Will rerun code in body to rebuild the object whenever a reactive value in the code changes.
Save the results to output$<outputId>

PREVENT REACTIONS
library(shiny)
ui <- fluidPage(
  textInput("a","","A"),
  textOutput("b")
)
server <-
function(input,output){
  output$b <-
    renderText({
      isolate({input$a})
    })
}
shinyApp(ui, server)

isolate(expr)
Runs a code block.
Returns a non-reactive copy of the results.

TRIGGER ARBITRARY CODE
library(shiny)
ui <- fluidPage(
  textInput("a","","A"),
  actionButton("go","Go")
)
server <-
function(input,output){
  observeEvent(input$go,{
    print(input$a)
  })
}
shinyApp(ui, server)

observeEvent(eventExpr, handlerExpr, event.env, event.quoted, handler.env, handler.quoted, label, suspended, priority, domain, autoDestroy, ignoreNULL)
Runs code in 2nd argument when reactive values in 1st argument change. See observe() for alternative.

MODULARIZE REACTIONS
ui <- fluidPage(
  textInput("a","","A"),
  textInput("z","","Z"),
  textOutput("b")
)
server <-
function(input,output){
  re <- reactive({
    paste(input$a, input$z)})
  output$b <- renderText({
    re()
  })
}
shinyApp(ui, server)

reactive(x, env, quoted, label, domain)
Creates a reactive expression that
· caches its value to reduce computation
· can be called by other code
· notifies its dependencies when it has been invalidated
Call the expression with function syntax, e.g. re()

DELAY REACTIONS
library(shiny)
ui <- fluidPage(
  textInput("a","","A"),
  actionButton("go","Go"),
  textOutput("b")
)
server <-
function(input,output){
  re <- eventReactive(
    input$go,{input$a})
  output$b <- renderText({
    re()
  })
}
shinyApp(ui, server)

eventReactive(eventExpr, valueExpr, event.env, event.quoted, value.env, value.quoted, label, domain, ignoreNULL)
Creates reactive expression with code in 2nd argument that only invalidates when reactive values in 1st argument change.

UI - An app's UI is an HTML document.
Use Shiny's functions to assemble this HTML with R.
fluidPage(
  textInput("a","")
)
Returns HTML

<label for="a">a</label>
<input id="a" type="text"
class="form-control" value=""/>

Add static HTML elements with tags, a list of functions that parallel common HTML tags, e.g. tags$a(). Unnamed arguments will be passed into the tag; named arguments will become tag attributes.

tags$a tags$data tags$h6 tags$nav tags$span
tags$abbr tags$datalist tags$head tags$noscript tags$strong
tags$address tags$dd tags$header tags$object tags$style
tags$area tags$del tags$hgroup tags$ol tags$sub
tags$article tags$details tags$hr tags$optgroup tags$summary
tags$aside tags$dfn tags$HTML tags$option tags$sup
tags$audio tags$div tags$i tags$output tags$table
tags$b tags$dl tags$iframe tags$p tags$tbody
tags$base tags$dt tags$img tags$param tags$td
tags$bdi tags$em tags$input tags$pre tags$textarea
tags$bdo tags$embed tags$ins tags$progress tags$tfoot
tags$blockquote tags$eventsource tags$kbd tags$q tags$th
tags$body tags$fieldset tags$keygen tags$ruby tags$thead
tags$br tags$figcaption tags$label tags$rp tags$time
tags$button tags$figure tags$legend tags$rt tags$title
tags$canvas tags$footer tags$li tags$s tags$tr
tags$caption tags$form tags$link tags$samp tags$track
tags$cite tags$h1 tags$mark tags$script tags$u
tags$code tags$h2 tags$map tags$section tags$ul
tags$colgroup tags$h3 tags$menu tags$select tags$var
tags$col tags$h4 tags$meta tags$small tags$video
tags$command tags$h5 tags$meter tags$source tags$wbr

The most common tags have wrapper functions. You do not need to prefix their names with tags$

ui <- fluidPage(
  h1("Header 1"),
  hr(),
  br(),
  p(strong("bold")),
  p(em("italic")),
  p(code("code")),
  a(href="", "Link"),
  HTML(" Raw html ")

Header 1
bold
italic
code
link
Raw html

To include a CSS file, use includeCSS(), or
1. Place the file in the www subdirectory
2. Link to it with
tags$head(tags$link(rel = "stylesheet", type = "text/css", href = "<file name>"))

To include JavaScript, use includeScript() or
1. Place the file in the www subdirectory
2. Link to it with
tags$head(tags$script(src = "<file name>"))

To include an image
1. Place the file in the www subdirectory
2. Link to it with img(src="<file name>")

Layouts
Combine multiple elements into a "single element" that has its own properties with a panel function, e.g.
wellPanel(dateInput("a", ""),
          submitButton()
)

absolutePanel() navlistPanel()
conditionalPanel() sidebarPanel()
fixedPanel() tabPanel()
headerPanel() tabsetPanel()
inputPanel() titlePanel()
mainPanel() wellPanel()

Organize panels and elements into a layout with a layout function. Add elements as arguments of the layout functions.

fluidRow()
ui <- fluidPage(
  fluidRow(column(width = 4),
    column(width = 2, offset = 3)),
  fluidRow(column(width = 12))
)

flowLayout()
ui <- fluidPage(
  flowLayout(# object 1,
    # object 2,
    # object 3
)
)

sidebarLayout()
side panel
ui <- fluidPage(
  sidebarLayout(
    sidebarPanel(),
    mainPanel()
)
)

splitLayout()
object 1
ui <- fluidPage(
  splitLayout(# object 1,
    # object 2
)
)

verticalLayout()
ui <- fluidPage(
  verticalLayout(# object 1,
    # object 2,
    # object 3
)
)

Layer tabPanels on top of each other, and navigate between them, with:
ui <- fluidPage(tabsetPanel(
  tabPanel("tab 1", contents),
  tabPanel("tab 2", contents),
  tabPanel("tab 3", contents)))

ui <- fluidPage(navlistPanel(
  tabPanel("tab 1", contents),
  tabPanel("tab 2", contents),
  tabPanel("tab 3", contents)))

ui <- navbarPage(title = "Page",
  tabPanel("tab 1", contents),
  tabPanel("tab 2", contents),
  tabPanel("tab 3", contents)))

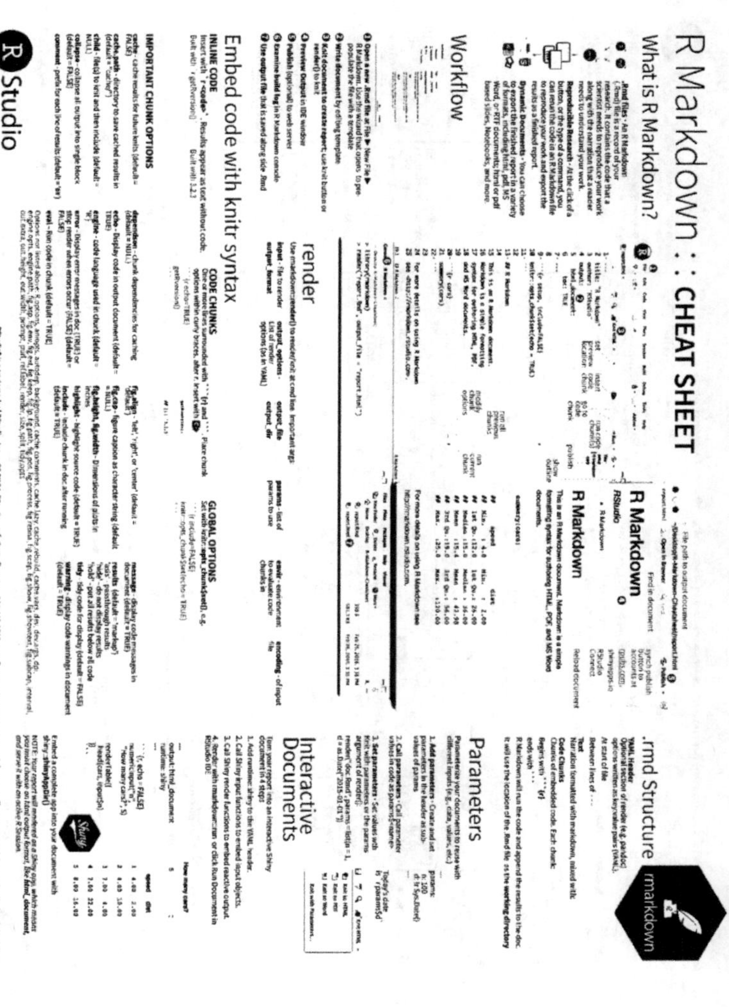

Pandoc's Markdown

Write with syntax on the left to create effect on right (after render)

Plain text	Plain text
End a line with two spaces to start a new paragraph.	End a line with two spaces to start a new paragraph.
italics and **bold**	*italics* and **bold**
`verbatim code`	`verbatim code`
sub/superscript^2^~2~	sub/superscript²₂
~~strikethrough~~	~~strikethrough~~
escaped: * _ \\	escaped: * _ \
endash: --, emdash: ---	endash: –, emdash: —
equation: $A = \pi*r^{2}$	equation: $A = \pi r^2$
equation block:	equation block:
$$E = mc^{2}$$	$E = mc^2$
> block quote	block quote
# Header1 {#anchor}	**Header1**
## Header 2 {#css_id}	**Header 2**
### Header 3 {.css_class}	**Header 3**
#### Header 4	**Header 4**
##### Header 5	**Header 5**
###### Header 6	**Header 6**
<!--Text comment-->	
\verb!Tex ignored in HTML!	TeX ignored in pdf
HTML ignored in pdfs	*HTML ignored in pdfs/emph*
<http://www.rstudio.com>	Jump to Header 1
[link](http://www.rstudio.com)	
Jump to [Header 1](#anchor)	
image:	image
`![Caption](smallorb.png)`	Caption

- unordered list
    + sub-item 1
    + sub-item 2
        - sub-sub-item 1
* item 2

Continued (indent 4 spaces)

1. ordered list
2. item 2
    i) sub-item 1
        A. sub-sub-item 1

(@) A list whose numbering continues after

(@) an interruption

Term 1

:   Definition 1

Right	Left	Default	Center
12	12	12	12
123	123	123	123
1	1	1	1

- slide bullet 1
- slide bullet 2

(> to have bullets appear on click)

Horizontal rule/slide break:

***

A footnote [^1]

[^1]: Here is the footnote

Set render options with YAML

When you render, R Markdown

1. runs the R code, embeds results and text into .md file with knitr
2. then converts the .md file into the finished format with pandoc

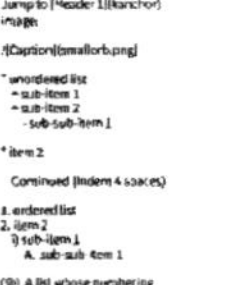

Set a document's default output format in the YAML header:

```
---
output: html_document
---

# Body
```

output value	creates
html_document	html
pdf_document	pdf (requires Tex)
word_document	Microsoft Word (.docx)
odt_document	OpenDocument Text
rtf_document	Rich Text Format
md_document	Markdown
github_document	Github compatible markdown
ioslides_presentation	ioslides HTML slides
slidy_presentation	slidy HTML slides
beamer_presentation	Beamer pdf slides (requires Tex)

Customize output with sub-options (listed to the right):

```
---
output: html_document:
  code_folding: hide
  toc_float: TRUE
---

# Body
```

html tabsets

Use tablet css class to place sub-headers into tabs

```
# Tabset {.tabset .tabset-fade .tabset-pills}
## Tab 1
text 1
## Tab 2
text 2
### End tabset
```

sub-option	description	html	pdf	word	odt	rtf	md	github	ioslides	slidy	beamer
citation_package	The LaTeX package to process citations, natbib, biblatex or none		X								X
code_folding	Let readers to toggle the display of R code, "none", "hide", or "show"	X									
colortheme	Beamer color theme to use										X
css	CSS file to use to style document	X							X	X	
dev	Graphics device to use for figure output (e.g. "png")	X	X	X	X	X	X		X	X	X
duration	Add a countdown timer (in minutes) to footer of slides								X		
fig_caption	Should figures be rendered with captions?	X	X	X	X				X	X	X
fig_height, fig_width	Default figure height and width (in inches) for document	X	X	X	X	X	X	X	X	X	X
highlight	Syntax highlighting: "tango", "pygments", "kate", "zenburn", "textmate"	X	X	X			X			X	X
includes	File of content to place in document (in_header, before_body, after_body)	X	X	X	X	X	X		X	X	X
incremental	Should bullets appear one at a time (on presenter mouse click)?								X	X	X
keep_md	Save a copy of .md file that contains knitr output	X		X	X		X	X		X	X
keep_tex	Save a copy of .tex file that contains knitr output		X								X
latex_engine	Engine to render latex, "pdflatex", "xelatex", or "lualatex"		X								X
lib_dir	Directory of dependency files to use (Bootstrap, MathJax, etc.)	X							X	X	
mathjax	Set to local or a URL to use a local/URL version of MathJax to render equations	X							X	X	
md_extensions	Markdown extensions to add to default definition or R Markdown	X	X	X	X	X	X	X	X	X	X
number_sections	Add section numbering to headers	X	X								
pandoc_args	Additional arguments to pass to Pandoc	X	X	X	X	X	X	X	X	X	X
preserve_yaml	Preserve YAML front matter in final document?							X			
reference_docx	docx file whose styles should be copied when producing docx output			X							
self_contained	Embed dependencies into the doc	X							X	X	
slide_level	The lowest heading level that defines individual slides										X
smaller	Use the smaller font size in the presentation?								X		
smart	Convert straight quotes to curly, dashes to em-dashes, … to ellipses, etc.	X							X	X	
template	Pandoc template to use when rendering file quarterly_report.html).	X	X			X			X		X
theme	Bootswatch or Beamer theme to use for page	X								X	
toc	Add a table of contents at start of document	X	X	X			X		X	X	X
toc_depth	The lowest level of headings to add to table of contents	X	X	X			X		X	X	X
toc_float	Float the table of contents to the left of the main content	X									

Create a Reusable Template

1. **Create a new package** with a inst/rmarkdown/templates directory

2. In the directory, **Place a folder** that contains:
   - **template.yaml** (see below)
   - **skeleton.Rmd** (contents of the template)
   - any supporting files

3. **Install the package**

4. **Access template** in wizard at File ▶ New File ▶ R Markdown

template.yaml

```
---
name: My Template
---
```

Table Suggestions

Several functions format R data into tables

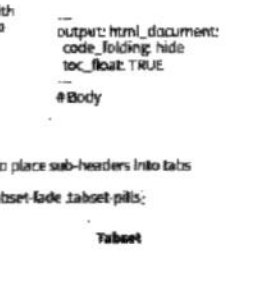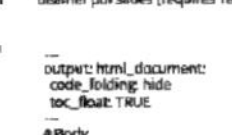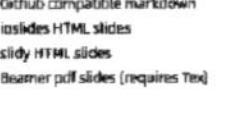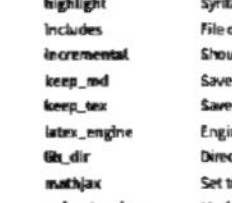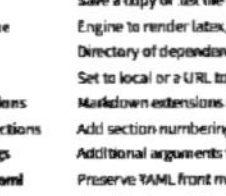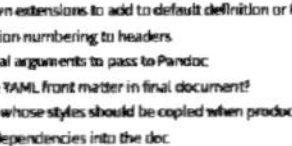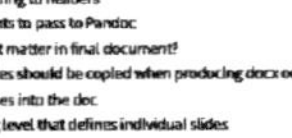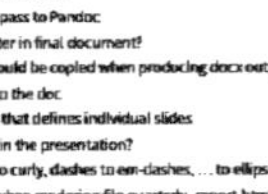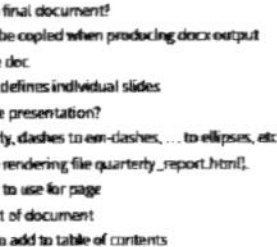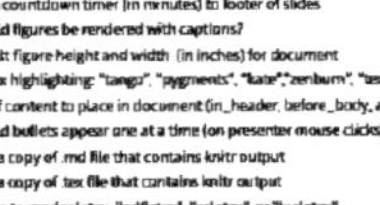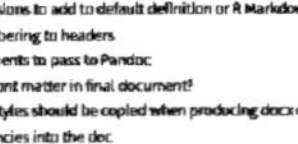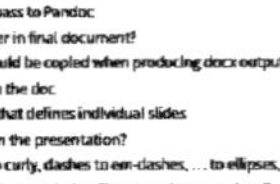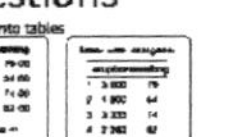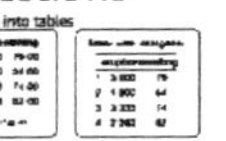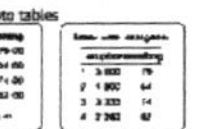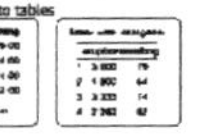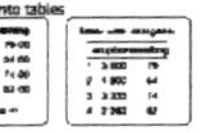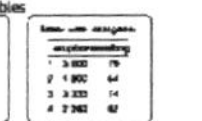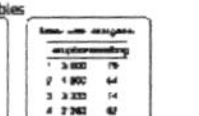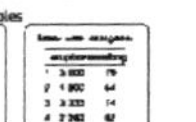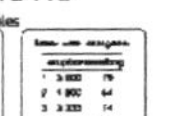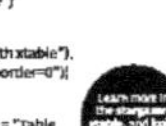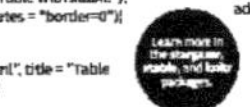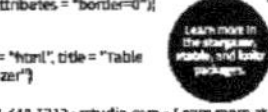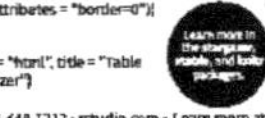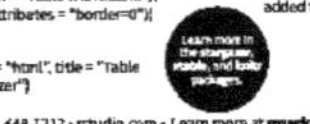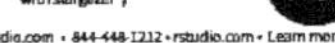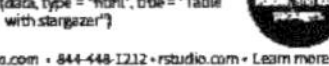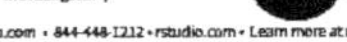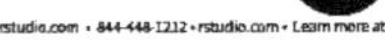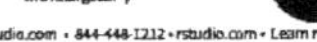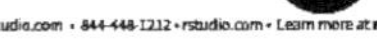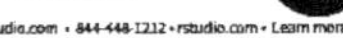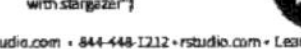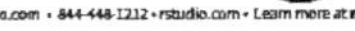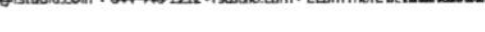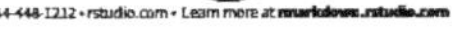

```
data <- faithful[1:4,]
```

```
```{r results = 'asis'}
knitr::kable(data, caption = "Table with kable")
```
```

```
```{r results = 'asis'}
print(xtable::xtable(data, caption = "Table with xtable"),
      type = "html", html.table.attributes = "border=0")
```
```

```
```{r results = 'asis'}
stargazer::stargazer(data, type = "html", title = "Table with stargazer")
```
```

Citations and Bibliographies

Create citations with .bib, .bibtex, .copac, .enl, .json, .medline, .mods, .ris, .wos, and .xml files

1. **Set bibliography file** and CSL 1.0 Style file (optional) in the YAML header

   bibliography: refs.bib
   csl: style.csl

2. **Use citation keys in text**

   Smith cited [@smith04].
   Smith cited without author [-@smith04].
   @smith04 cited in line.

3. **Render.** Bibliography will be added to end of document

   Smith cited Lore Smith 2004.
   Smith cited without author (2004).
   Joe Smith (2004) cited in line.

R Studio